Walks in Literary
SANTA FE

No other town of its size in America has been the subject of and focus for as much good literature as Santa Fe. . . . Looked at in one way, Santa Fe was a mud village. In another way, it was the solitary oasis of human picturesqueness in a continent of vacancy. Like that of Athens, though of an entirely different quality, its fame was out of all proportion to its size.

— J. Frank Dobie (1888–1964)
Guide to Life and Literature of the Southwest (1952)

Walks in Literary
SANTA FE

A Guide to Landmarks, Legends, and Lore

BARBARA HARRELSON

Gibbs Smith, Publisher

TO ENRICH AND INSPIRE HUMANKIND

Salt Lake City | Charleston | Santa Fe | Santa Barbara

First Edition
11 10 09 08 07   5 4 3 2 1

Text © 2007 Barbara J. Harrelson
Photographs credited on page 121

Cover Art:
   Gustave Baumann, *Old Santa Fe, 1924,* color woodcut.
   Collection of the Museum of Fine Arts, New Mexico.
   Gift of the School of American Research, 1952.
   © Ann Baumann

Published by
Gibbs Smith, Publisher
PO Box 667
Layton, Utah 84041

1.800.835.4993 orders
www.gibbs-smith.com

Designed by Linda Herman
Printed and bound in China

Library of Congress Cataloging-in-Publication Data

Harrelson, Barbara.
  Walks in literary Santa Fe : a guide to landmarks,
legends, and lore / Barbara Harrelson. — 1st ed.
       p. cm.
  Includes bibliographical references and index.
  ISBN-13: 978-1-4236-0182-1
  ISBN-10: 1-4236-0182-3
  1. Literary landmarks—New Mexico—Santa Fe.
  2. Walking—New Mexico—Santa Fe—Guidebooks.
  I. Title.

PS144.N35H37 2007
917.89'56—dc22   2006029881

To my mother, Jodie Beckett,
who introduced me to the love of stories;

୧୨

to my teacher, Edwin Leupold,
who encouraged me to write;

୧୨

and to my friend and mentor, Miriam Grant.

Contents

ଔ

Acknowledgments   viii

Foreword   ix

Introduction   x

Downtown Santa Fe (#1)   2

 1   The Plaza   4

 2   The Palace of the Governors   15

 3   Fray Angélico Chávez History Library   22

 4   Prince and Sena Plazas   26

 5   Museum of the Institute of American Indian Arts   31

 6   Cathedral Basilica of St. Francis of Assisi   33

 7   La Fonda Hotel   39

 8   Burro Alley   44

 9   Lensic Theater   47

10   Santa Fe River Walk   49

11   The Loretto Chapel   50

    Downtown Bookstores

    B1 Palace Gift Shop   21

    B2 Nicholas Potter Bookseller   31

    B3 La Fonda Hotel Newsstand   39

    B4 Collected Works Bookstore   46

Old Santa Fe Trail to Canyon Road (#2)   52

 1   Barrio de Analco   54

 2   San Miguel Mission Chapel   55

 3   New Mexico Capitol   57

4	Witter Bynner's Home (Inn of the Turquoise Bear)	59
5	Arroyo Tenorio to Acequia Madre	64
6	Acequia Madre to Camino del Monte Sol	65
7	Mary Austin's Home (Chiaroscuro Contemporary Art)	67
8	Will Shuster's Home	74
9	Acequia Madre and Don Miguel	77
10	Gerald Cassidy Placita	80
11	Canyon Road	81
12	El Zaguán	82
13	Adolph Bandelier's Home (Sherwood's Spirit of America Gallery)	84

Bookstores
B1 Garcia Street Books *and* Downtown Subscription 65

Resources 85

New Mexico Literary Timeline 86
Taos Literary Landmarks 95
Publishers, Booksellers, and Literary Resources 98
Writers' Workshops, Conferences, and Retreats 108
New Mexico Literary Classics
and Other Recommended Books 110
Bibliography 118

Image Credits 121
Index 122

Acknowledgments

I AM INDEBTED TO MANY FRIENDS, colleagues, and scholars for help in developing the literary walking tour that inspired this book. Layne Vickers Smith first planted the seed for a guidebook to literary Santa Fe. Saul Cohen, Orlando Romero, Ellen Bradbury-Reid, and Peggy van Hulsteyn were generous with their expertise as I began to create the format and content of the tour.

Robert Gish has provided valuable insight and guidance; I have relied on several of his books on literary New Mexicans and Southwest literature. Robert Frost has given generously of his time and knowledge at frequent visits to the Inn of the Turquoise Bear, the former home of Witter Bynner. Nick Potter and Andre Dumont have shared their enthusiasm for Southwest literature, showing many of the treasured volumes in their respective collections of used and rare books.

Candelora Versace and Dorothy Doyle, two of the greatest promoters of Southwest literature, have provided both inspiration and sound advice. Kay and Willard Lewis have given support and perspective through their love of Southwest literature and Santa Fe's historic landmarks and neighborhoods.

In my research for this book, I am grateful to the knowledgeable and gracious staff at the Fray Angélico Chávez History Library and the Photo Archives of the Palace of the Governors, especially Tomas Jaehn, Hazel Romero, Daniel Kosharek, and Cary McStay. Special thanks to Ann Baumann and the Gustave Baumann estate for permission to use the color woodcut of *Old Santa Fe, 1924* on the cover—and to Michelle Roberts at the Museum of Fine Arts for her assistance. And, a huge thank you to Ellen Kleiner at Ancient City Press/Gibbs Smith, Publisher, for helping the book become a reality.

Foreword

SANTA FE IS FAMOUS FOR MANY THINGS—adobes, sunsets, artists, music, food, and more—but its literary history, just as illustrious as some of its other attributes, is not as well known. Here is an antidote to that situation: Barbara Harrelson has written a little history of Santa Fe's authors, past and present.

A surprising number of very well-known authors visited Santa Fe, and some stayed. Others, lured by the powerful Mabel Dodge Luhan, were drawn to Taos. There is a funny story about Mabel Dodge (before Luhan) meeting Alice Corbin Henderson (already a queen of the Santa Fe scene). Mabel was (always) late and when she arrived for tea at the Hendersons (late), Alice Corbin scolded her. Mabel confided in her diary, "I certainly did not come to Santa Fe to be fussed at by a woman from Chicago." (Mabel was from Buffalo.)

Clearly the town was not big enough for both of them. But it held many others who wrote and gossiped and drank their collective way though many evenings.

The artists always said it was the light, but for the writers it must have been the wealth of material and the distance from their East Coast agents.

This guidebook is enjoyable, and if you take the walks, you will really delight in the information as well as the scenery. Happy literary walks . . .

— Ellen Bradbury-Reid,
the author of several books,
is founder of the Southwest Literary Center
and executive director of Recursos de Santa Fe.

Introduction

A LITERARY WALKING TOUR OF SANTA FE surveys this "Creative City" through its stories and its authors, past and present.★ The histories of Santa Fe and its peoples, recorded in many ways over the past four centuries, comprise the warp of the literary tapestry. The folklore, legends, and stories—with threads from each of the three dominant cultures: Native American, Hispanic, and Anglo-American—complete the weft of the richly woven literary heritage of Santa Fe.

This guidebook offers a different way of experiencing Santa Fe's literature and history, complementary to reading the books. The literary walks present familiar landmarks by emphasizing associated stories and authors. Santa Fe's historic and legendary figures are revealed in new ways through the prism of story. The region's history, architecture, and cultural traditions are the context for the narratives that are center stage in this guided tour.

Two literary walks are described, with accompanying maps, photos, and illustrations. (Numbers on the maps are keyed to textual descriptions of the sites.) **Downtown Santa Fe (#1)** surveys the area surrounding the central plaza, with popular landmarks assuming literary connotations. The **Old Santa Fe Trail and Canyon Road (#2)** follows the colorful paths along Canyon Road and the adjacent residential neighborhoods encompassing Acequia Madre and Camino del Monte Sol, where many artists and writers resided in the past. (Note: a few of the homes of historic Santa Fe writers are still private residences; therefore, only a general reference to the neighborhood in which each lived is given.)

★ In 2005, Santa Fe became the first North American city to be designated a "Creative City" by UNESCO (United Nations Educational, Scientific, and Cultural Organization). The goal is to promote cultural diversity and creative industries around the world through a Creative Cities Network.

Walking times will vary according to your pace and interests but need never exceed two hours. Suggested stops for refreshment and book browsing are indicated, with selected bookstores noted on the maps.

Narrative "interludes" between sites that give background and context are designated with this symbol: **ᏼ**. Sidebars (or boxes) scattered throughout the book contain book titles, author quotes, and book excerpts to supplement the text. Resource material includes book lists, a New Mexico literary timeline, and a directory of local publishers, booksellers, and literary organizations.

Why a literary walking tour of Santa Fe? Because Santa Fe's impressive narrative arts and literary lights are beginning to gain the attention they deserve, along with the city's visual and performing arts. Many Santa Fe–based writers, poets, playwrights, and screenwriters, some with international reputations, are producing literature and media arts unrivaled by any other artistic center of comparable size.

Only a handful of literary walking tours remains in the United States—notably in the Greater Boston area, New York's Greenwich Village, Key West, and San Francisco. Santa Fe's designation as a world-class cultural destination in the early '90s has attracted an increasing number of sophisticated travelers who want to pursue the distinctive arts and culture of the region. Santa Fe's economy—and New Mexico's—gets a big boost from such cultural tourism.

Storytelling in Santa Fe continues today as a vital force and everyday occurrence, reflecting both tradition and innovation in the literature of the region. Today, as always, the spirit of place is paramount in the literature, whether a crime novel set in an urban setting, a coming-of-age story set in a village steeped in tradition, or a focus on the land and water rights issues that dominate recent fiction and nonfiction alike. The storytellers in our history range from the ancient native peoples with their spoken narratives and songs to contemporary poets (rap and traditional), novelists, and science writers who use a computer and the World Wide Web.

Some of the names of Santa Fe authors are easily recognized: Michael McGarrity, Sallie Bingham, Evan Connell, Bob Mayer, Hampton Sides, Frederick Turner, Sarah Lovett, and Cormac McCarthy. Even our "resident actors," like Gene Hackman, Ali MacGraw, and Alan Arkin, are writing books and participating in local literary events.

The city council named Santa Fe's first poet laureate in 2006, recognizing the talents and contributions of Arthur Sze. He has published eight poetry books and recently retired after twenty-two years of teaching at the Institute of American Indian Arts (IAIA), where he founded the school's Bachelor of Fine Arts degree in creative writing.

Three men whose bodies of work designate them as "elders" of New Mexico letters are Tony Hillerman, N. Scott Momaday, and Rudolfo Anaya. Each has strong Santa Fe affiliations and appears here regularly, although none lives here now. They are revered for distinctive books that represent their respective backgrounds yet have universal appeal. You will learn more about these acclaimed writers, and more, as you walk Santa Fe's literary trails.

You will also become acquainted (or reacquainted) with their predecessors who came to Santa Fe and Taos in the 1920s and 1930s, producing a Golden Age of Arts and Letters along with their artist counterparts in the City of Holy Faith. Alice Corbin Henderson, Witter Bynner, Mary Austin, Oliver La Farge, Ruth Laughlin, Paul Horgan, Fray Angélico Chávez, Erna Fergusson, and Willa Cather, among others—their legacy abounds in Santa Fe today. The Taos artists and writers of that era mingled often with those in Santa Fe; the literary walks include references to Mabel Dodge Luhan, D. H. Lawrence, Willard "Spud" Johnson, and Frank Waters, among others. (Notes on literary landmarks in Taos are part of the Resources section of this guidebook.)

A directory of New Mexico writers compiled from 1930s sources appeared in the 1982 book *Santa Fe and Taos: The Writer's Era, 1916–1941*, by Marta Weigle and Kyle Fiore. Some 320 writers are listed, with slightly more than one-third of them identified with Santa Fe.

Today, I have estimated at least one hundred writers are living in Santa Fe part-time or year-round, but it is impossible to track them all, with new bylines appearing almost daily. Clearly, it is a high per-capita ratio, given Santa Fe's population of about 68,000.

What is it about Santa Fe—and New Mexico—that has attracted creative people from the world over, particularly since the early twentieth century? Enchantment, mystique, and magic are the words most often used to describe the "spell" of this region. Drawn by the natural beauty and the cultural richness, many come here for a taste of life in the not-so-fast lane, fall in love with it, and stay to reinvent themselves, a characteristically American pursuit.

Santa Fe Style, a cliché applied to design, architecture, clothing, and cuisine, also describes the diversity and eccentricity that define this city today. A unique outlook flourishes here that cherishes the past while inviting exploration and invention.

It is no accident that the New York–based touring production of Homer's *The Iliad* and *The Odyssey* played to sold-out crowds during exclusive engagements here in the summer of 2006. A look at *Pasatiempo*, the weekly arts and leisure supplement of the *Santa Fe New Mexican*, confirms that Santa Feans experience the best of the arts year-round—and that many of us are producing it as well.

This guidebook has been developed as a comprehensive overview of Santa Fe's literary heritage and current activities, with enough documentation to inform the narrative—but it is by no means an exhaustive or scholarly survey. With new authors, books, and literary events emerging almost daily in Santa Fe, this guidebook, like the literary walking tour that inspired it, has been a work in progress. My hope is that it will be an entertaining and useful Baedeker of Santa Fe books and authors, past and present.

The chief glory of every people arises from its authors.
—Samuel Johnson (1709–1784)

DOWNTOWN SANTA FE

OLD SANTA FE TRAIL TO CANYON ROAD

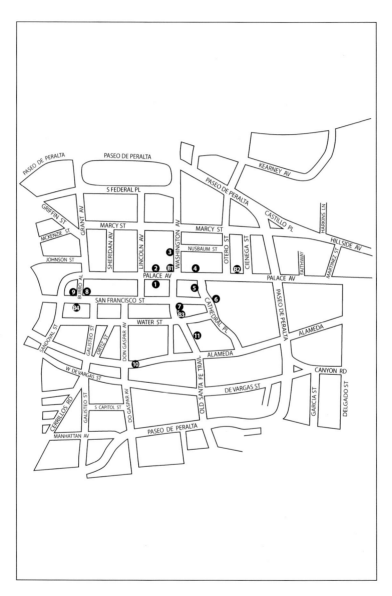

DOWNTOWN SANTA FE

⊂⊗

1 The Plaza

2 Palace of the Governors

   B1 *Palace Gift Shop* (books)

3 Fray Angélico Chávez
History Library

4 Prince and Sena Plazas

   B2 *Nicholas Potter Bookseller*

5 Museum of the
Institute of American
Indian Arts

6 Cathedral Basilica of
St. Francis of Assisi

7 La Fonda Hotel

   B3 *La Fonda Newsstand*

8 Burro Alley

   B4 *Collected Works Bookstore*

9 Lensic Theater

10 Santa Fe River Walk

11 The Loretto Chapel

Note: Entrance fees are required at the Palace of the Governors, Institute of American Indian Arts Museum, and the Loretto Chapel. No tour groups are allowed inside the Cathedral Basilica of St. Francis.

DOWNTOWN SANTA FE

THE PLAZA

THE WALK IN DOWNTOWN SANTA FE begins and ends at **The Plaza (1)**, the heart (*el corazón*) of Santa Fe today as it was at the beginning. La Villa Real de Santa Fe (the Royal City of Holy Faith) was laid out in the traditional Spanish design in 1609–1610, with the first structures surrounding a central square (or rectangle, as it was then), the *plaza mayor*. The Palace of the Governors (the executive offices and residence), soldiers' barracks, a parish church, a few businesses, and some residences around the Plaza constituted downtown Santa Fe. In territorial days, a wooden bandstand stood in the center of the Plaza; it was replaced by the soldiers' monument (obelisk) that still stands there today.

For four hundred years, the Santa Fe Plaza has witnessed the parade of history through five changes in government—from early Spanish rule to statehood in 1912. Community proclamations, religious processions, markets, and fiestas have occupied its space, along with public floggings, cockfights—and the "first American Revolution," when the Pueblo Revolt of 1680 succeeded in driving the Spanish out of Santa Fe.[1] When the Spanish returned in 1693, most of the settlement around the Plaza had to be rebuilt; only the Palace survived.

The Santa Fe Plaza speaks of beginnings and endings, past and prologue. The oldest capital city in the United States, Santa Fe was founded about 1607 (historians disagree about the actual date). It

---

[1] The Pueblo Revolt of 1680 is the name generally used to describe this historical event, but many Native Americans do not use it because they believe that the name itself reflects a biased view of events. They would say that a more accurate term is revolution. Pueblo Independence Day is celebrated on August 10, the day that the Pueblo Revolt of 1680 began, or on any of the days through August 13.

was established as the capital of *la Nueva México*, the northernmost region of viceregal New Spain. More than two centuries later, beginning in 1821, the Plaza marked the end of the nine-hundred-mile journey across the Santa Fe Trail from Missouri. It was also the terminus for the Camino Real (Royal Road), connecting Santa Fe to Mexico City—a vital link during the Spanish Colonial years. Santa Fe and its Plaza remained at the nexus of these great trade routes until the coming of the railroad in 1880 created a new economy and a new era.

Today, the downtown Plaza hosts community gatherings, musical concerts, several major art markets and crafts fairs—and individuals who want to enjoy the sunset or a winter snowfall.

The Fourth of July in Santa Fe means a pancake breakfast on the Plaza (to benefit the United Way) and a display of vintage automobiles from around the country. Mid-August brings about one hundred thousand visitors from around the world to the annual Santa Fe Indian Market to buy original art directly from some twelve hundred artists. The weekend after Labor Day, residents flock to the Plaza in celebration of the annual Santa Fe Fiesta, the oldest community celebration still in existence.

Any book with a Santa Fe setting is certain to mention the Plaza, but one book that makes it a central character is ***Ride the Pink Horse*** (1946), by **Dorothy B. Hughes** (1904–1993). She was one of the nation's most prominent woman authors of mystery and detective fiction in the '40s and '50s. Born in Kansas City, Dorothy Belle Flanagan Hughes lived in Albuquerque and Santa Fe, where she was also a respected journalist and critic. Three of her novels were turned into major motion pictures.

Ride the Pink Horse refers to the colorful carousel named Tio Vivo that used to appear on the Plaza every year during the annual Santa

Revelers dance in the streets around the Plaza during the Santa Fe Fiesta, 1938.

Fe Fiesta. La Fonda Hotel and other downtown sites also play key roles in this novel that became a movie by the same name. Unfortunately, the 1947 film has not been reproduced for home viewing. The two other Hughes novels that became movies are *The Fallen Sparrow* (1943) and *In a Lonely Place* (1950).

03

Storytelling Traditions of Three Peoples

Find a park bench and enjoy one of Santa Fe's (mostly) sunny days with brisk clean air. Here is a good vantage point to reflect on the origins of storytelling in this part of the world.

The first contributors to the literature of this place were the **indigenous peoples** who inhabited the Four Corners area and the

Rio Grande valley for centuries before any Europeans arrived. These Native Americans celebrated and transmitted their tribal stories, songs, myths, and rituals primarily through the spoken word, with the elders passing on family wisdom from generation to generation. In fact they still believe that the most sacred stories and songs must be passed on only through spoken words and never written down. This tradition poses a conundrum for many modern Indians (note: they call themselves both "Indians" and "Native Americans") who no longer speak their native tongues and are trying to preserve their languages and stories by transcribing them into written language.

N. Scott Momaday, the highly respected Native American writer with roots in New Mexico, has said: "American literature begins with the first human perception of the American landscape expressed and preserved in language." (Essay: "The Native Voice," in *The Columbia Literary History of the United States*, 1988.) Momaday has devoted much of his life to preserving the oral tradition of his people. (Momaday and his work are discussed at (5) on the map of this walk.)

Early stories and myths were also depicted graphically through the petroglyphs and pictographs (rock art) still found in areas near Santa Fe and elsewhere in the Southwest. Even the tribal dances and sacred sand paintings may be seen as modes of story as well as ritual.

Yes, these ancient peoples had a literary tradition but it did not involve what we call books, with words written on paper. Their relatives in pre-Columbian Mesoamerica, however, did have a kind of bark paper, *amate*, made from the mulberry tree. Paper was important in the religious practices of Mesoamerica and valued by the Aztecs, along with precious stones, metals, and feathers. Books made of this paper contained cutout figures representing spirits or gods.

With the Spanish conquest of Mexico in the early sixteenth century, papermaking and ritualistic paper cutting went underground because authorities made it illegal to own paper. Any "books" that were found were destroyed by the Franciscan friars, who deemed them works of the devil. The beliefs associated with the rituals prevailed and those lost paper arts are being revived in Mexico today. (The Palace of the Governors presented a Santa Fe workshop called "Paper Soul: Indigenous Bookcrafts of Mexico" in the summer of 2006.)

The second people to inhabit this part of the world, adding to its literary heritage, were the **Spanish**. Noted local historian and author **Marc Simmons** points out that the first books brought into New Mexico were likely religious volumes, missals, and devotional books carried by clerics, such as Fray Marcos de Niza who came here in 1539, and the five friars accompanying the Coronado expedition in 1540. (From his 1976 essay on "Authors and Books in Colonial New Mexico" in *Voices from the Southwest: A Gathering of Poetry, Essays, and Art in Honor of Lawrence Clark Powell*.)

"So it is reasonable to assume that the first printed volume ever opened and read under New Mexico's shining turquoise sky was one of sacred content; and, in fact, all evidence available suggests that throughout Spanish times, the majority of books brought here pertained to religion," Simmons concludes.

The officers among the conquistadors who came with Cortés and Pizarro were undoubtedly literate men who believed in the power of the pen as well as the sword. The printing press had been invented in Europe in 1455 and, despite Spain's isolation, it is likely that early printed books would have found their way into the educated classes by the time of the Spanish explorations in the early sixteenth century. The rank-and-file Spanish soldier may have been

Captain Gaspar Pérez de Villagrá wrote the first epic poem about New Mexico, published in Spain in 1610.

illiterate or barely literate, but the Franciscan friars who traveled with them would have provided assistance with letter writing and devotional materials.

In fact, the Spanish officials and administrators, both at home and abroad, were sticklers for documentation, requiring that multiple copies be executed of all records. This habit proved a boon to history when the Pueblo Revolt of 1680 destroyed most of the government and church records in Santa Fe. Scholars have been able to find copies of important documents in various libraries and repositories in Spain and Mexico.

The first epic poem written about New Mexico was ***Historia de la Nueva México*** by **Captain Gaspar Pérez de Villagrá**, one of Juan de Oñate's officers in the 1598 expedition. Written in blank verse and published in Spain in 1610, it "tells of the slow, painful journey of Oñate's colonists up the Rio Grande, the founding of a first capital at San Juan Pueblo, and the bloody war waged against the Acoma Indians," wrote **Adolph Bandelier**.

Bandelier (1840–1914), the pioneering Swiss-American anthropologist and novelist who explored the ruins in 1880 now named for him, is also discussed at other sites on the Santa Fe literary walks. His home is part of the Canyon Road Walk, while his collected papers reside in the Fray Angélico Chávez History Library, part of this walk. (Bandelier National Monument is forty minutes from Santa Fe.)

According to Marc Simmons ("Authors and Books in Colonial New Mexico"), "Bandelier discovered the *Historia* when he was doing research at Mexico's National Museum in the early 1890s. For him, it was an eye opener, filling in what was then a yawning gap in the early history of New Mexico."

Bandelier's assessment of the epic poem was, Simmons says, "sympathetic to its merits and conscious of its obvious shortcomings." In Bandelier's words, *"The book contains very heavy, nay clumsy, poetry. Still it is exceedingly valuable. Villagrá was an execrable poet, but a reliable historian so far as he saw and took part in the events himself. His narration of the tragedy at Acoma and of the recapture of the pueblo is too Homeric altogether; but in this he followed the style of the period."*

From that "Homeric" epic, the Spanish colonial literary thread winds its way through an era encompassing the Pueblo Revolt of 1680 and the reconquest of Santa Fe in 1693. The Spanish were able to regain control only after they agreed to concessions. In order to live peacefully with the Pueblo peoples (and the Apaches who had joined in the revolution), Spanish leaders agreed to end policies of forced labor and tribute, to recognize native land claims, and to allow the practices of native religion—provided that the Indians allowed missionaries into their villages and agreed to practice Catholicism as well.

When Jesus Came, the Corn Mothers Went Away (1991), by **Ramón Gutiérrez**, is an excellent text describing the cultural

READ MORE ABOUT . . .

THE PUEBLO REVOLT OF 1680

- From *Red Power on the Rio Grande: The Native American Revolution of 1680,*★ by **Franklin Folsom** (published in 1973), the late Alfonso Ortiz, San Juan Pueblo, wrote in the book's Introduction: "This revolution was fought for precisely the same reasons that the revolution of 1776 was fought—to regain freedom from tyranny, persecution, and unjust taxation. Only this native revolution was fought in 1680, ninety-six years before there was an America."

- *Taos: A Novel*, by **Irwin R. Blacker**, is a 1959 fiction account of the 1680 revolt. Although it is out of print, copies are easily found. According to Santa Fe attorney, author, and bibliophile Saul Cohen, "It has a Tolstoyan sweep, and the characters, Indian and Spanish, are human beings."

- *Serafina's Stories,* by **Rudolfo Anaya** (published in 2004) is a collection of tales (*cuentos*) narrated within a historical framework that attempts to explain the circumstances that led to the 1680 revolt and, in the telling, to heal old wounds. In this New Mexico version of Scheherazade, a young Indian woman named Serafina entices the governor with stories and wins the freedom of Indian prisoners, including one based on Popé, the San Juan Pueblo medicine man credited with leading the uprising.

★ The book was republished in 1998 with a new title: *Indian Uprising on the Rio Grande: The Pueblo Revolt of 1680.*

shifts in Native American religious practices that were established in eighteenth-century New Mexico—and continue today.

In 1821, Mexico won its independence from Spain, and Santa Fe (and New Mexico) became part of the Republic of Mexico. This brought significant change because the Mexicans opened up the province to trade and commerce from outside its borders—something that Spain had refused to do, imposing a harsh isolation on the colony in order to preserve sovereignty.

In that same year, the first wagons from Missouri arrived in Santa Fe, bringing goods and new influences over the Santa Fe Trail. The **Americans, or Anglos** (non-Indian, non-Hispanic/Mexican) are the third group of people to influence the literature of this region. They began coming to this "foreign" land in greater numbers in search of prosperity, adventure, and a new life.

The books, journals, and letters written by these Manifest Destiny pioneers provide the third literary thread in Santa Fe's cultural tapestry. These writings record some of the first impressions of Santa Fe by "white people."

The picture painted by these initial reports was often not positive; in fact, many of these visitors saw shabby mud houses, poverty, and ignorance ("the natives don't speak English") in the Royal City. Others were able to appreciate its rustic charms and the grandeur of its physical surroundings. Then, as now, Santa Fe inspired extremes of emotion but rarely indifference.

Two memoirs by women are perennial favorites: **Marian Sloan Russell** describes her journey west at age seven in *Land of Enchantment: Memoirs of Marian Russell Along the Santa Fe Trail: As Dictated to Mrs. Hal Russell* (first published 1954, reprinted 1985); *Down the Santa Fe Trail and into Mexico: The Diary of Susan Shelby Magoffin, 1846–47* was published in 1846, reprinted in 1926 and 1982. Susan Magoffin was an eighteen-year-old bride when she traveled the Santa Fe Trail.

INSPIRED BY SANTA FE

Writers have recorded their impressions of Santa Fe from its early days to the present. These narrative pictures reflect varied perspectives—but rarely indifference.

The drowsy old town, lying in a sandy valley inclosed [sic] on three sides by mountain walls, is built of adobes laid in one-story houses, and resembles an extensive brick-yard, with scattered sunburnt kilns ready for the fire. . . . Yet, dirty and unkept, swarming with hungry dogs, it has the charm of foreign flavor, and, like San Antonio, retains some portion of the grace which long lingers about, if indeed it ever forsakes, the spot where Spain has held rule for centuries, and the soft syllables of the Spanish tongue are yet heard.

— Susan Elston Wallace, *The Land of the Pueblos* (1888)

இஇ

Biographers of Santa Fe, with notable exception of the late Oliver La Farge, have been inclined to talk of her in terms of externals. They describe narrow, aimless streets; the softness of adobe buildings, lilacs, and the long, red sunsets which flood the cranky old city with gaudy colors. All this is there. The City of the Holy Faith has been growing in its spectacular and impractical mountain setting since 1610 and it shows both its age and its Spanish-Colonial origins. But the real essence of Santa Fe is invisible and can't be communicated through adjectives. It has something to do with the best of the women's clubs formally naming itself "The Stitch and Bitch," something to do with the good-natured insolence of plaza shoeshine boys, and something to do with the cynical civic attitude toward growth and progress—which Santa Feans view with no more enthusiasm than a milking goat has for cold hands. It has something to do with lethargy and with tolerance

(Cont'd on next page)

(Inspired by Santa Fe, cont'd)

(symptoms, perhaps, of old age). Most of all, it has something to do with people. . . . Santa Fe celebrates the individual.

— Tony Hillerman, from "The Conversion of Cletus Xywanda,"
The Great Taos Bank Robbery and Other Indian Country Affairs (1973)

❧

Along with San Francisco and New Orleans, Santa Fe is one of the most humane of all American cities; by some miracle it has so far managed to ban the skyscraper, and the literal low profile there extends to other things. . . . Perhaps because it has opted out of the high-rise ratrace, and has attracted a huge art-and-crafts colony, Santa Fe is noticeably relaxed; provincial, perhaps, but proud of it. The Spanish Colonial adobe buildings with their pretty patios, the sweet-pungent incense of the piñón logs that pervades every New Mexican dusk, the marvelous light and air of the high desert, the cottonwoods, the old colonnaded shops around the sleepy central plaza, the cathedral bells chiming through the night . . . it's not at all the America of the European myth, and I liked it very much that first time, and have not changed my mind since.

— John Fowles, *Daniel Martin* (1977)

Commerce of the Prairies, by **Josiah Gregg,** appeared in 1844 (reprinted in 1954 and 1990) and remains a classic. Gregg, a trader and trailblazer, made repeated trips along the Santa Fe Trail. He is credited with bringing the first printing press into the territory in 1834.

The first book to be printed in New Mexico was the ***Cuaderno de Ortigrafía***, a school spelling primer, published in 1835 by **Padre Antonio José Martínez**, the curate of Taos. The original copy of the *Cuaderno* now lives in the Fray Angélico Chávez History Library behind the Palace of the Governors, the next two stops on the walk.

The Palace of the Governors, the oldest public building in the United States, is decked in evergreens for Christmas celebrations, 1985.

THE PALACE OF THE GOVERNORS

RESUME THE WALK by turning to **The Palace of the Governors (2)**. Built about 1610, the Palace was the first official seat of the government, combining the residence of the governor with administrative offices and outlying buildings for a military garrison and a stockade. It was built of adobe in the Spanish hacienda style with an interior *placita* (courtyard).

The oldest public building still in use in the United States, the Palace has dominated the Plaza throughout Santa Fe's history. Since 1909, it has served as the History Museum of the Museum of New Mexico.

A new History Museum is under construction behind the Palace of the Governors, scheduled to open on Memorial Day 2008. The

Palace and its present exhibition spaces will be reconfigured to showcase particular objects and collections.

Spend some time in the Palace where New Mexico's history comes alive. The Indian vendors under the *portal* (portico) compete for the highly prized positions to sell their goods, which are certified by the Museum to be authentic.

From the literary perspective, the Palace was home to two territorial governors who were authors, **Lew Wallace** and **Bradford Prince**. (**Miguel Antonio Otero**, who was the first Hispano to serve as governor of New Mexico Territory, wrote several volumes of memoirs, but did not live in the Palace during his term because it had fallen into disrepair.)

Wallace is probably the most famous of these authors, known for his successful novel ***Ben Hur: A Tale of the Christ***, published in 1880. He completed the book while living in the Palace of the Governors; his chair and writing table are part of the museum's collection.

Those who remember the 1959 film *Ben Hur*, with Charlton Heston (and the famous chariot race), may wonder what this story has to do with Santa Fe or New Mexico. Simply the accident of time and place of authorship explains how *Ben Hur* came to be a part of this walk.

Lewis "Lew" Wallace (1827–1905) was a native of Indiana, where he was admitted to the bar and served in the state senate. He distinguished himself as one of the youngest generals in the Union Army during the Civil War. His father had been governor of Indiana, but Lew found that he did not have much appetite for politics, although he filled important public service positions during his career. Art, music, and literature were the pursuits that he favored. Wallace was a man of letters, first as a journalist and then as an author and biographer. In addition to *Ben Hur*, he wrote *The Fair God* (1873) and *The*

A bird's-eye view of Santa Fe (1882) reflects the town about the time that Lew Wallace was New Mexico's territorial governor.

Life of Gen. Ben Harrison (1888), as well as *Lew Wallace: An Autobiography*, published posthumously in 1906.

His wife, **Susan Elston Wallace**, was also a writer and authored a book about their time in New Mexico Territory. ***The Land of the Pueblos***, published in 1888, is part memoir, part travelogue.

Lew Wallace's tenure as governor of New Mexico Territory (1878–1881) was filled with enough challenge, intrigue, and discomfort to daunt many a leader—he and his wife, Susan, came to regard it as a "hardship post" and were happy when they could move on. (Susan wrote to their son in 1879, saying that she agreed with General Sherman—we should have another war with Mexico and make them take back New Mexico.)

Wallace had been appointed in 1878 by President Rutherford B. Hayes to reform the corruption and disarray in New Mexico's government that had been the norm for years. Hayes declared Lincoln County (in southeast New Mexico) to be in a state of insurrection and sent in a "pro" to restore order.

The Colfax County War (1875–1878) and the Lincoln County War (1878–1881) involved the Wild West's version of the robber barons, along with cattle rustlers, outlaws, and dishonest officials "on the take." It was no Gilded Age in this part of the country; in fact, New Mexico Territory was described as being "as dangerous a country as ever lay out of doors" (attributed to Emerson Hough in John H. Vaughn's *History and Government of New Mexico*, privately printed in 1931).

Billy the Kid and the **Santa Fe Ring** were among those challenges that Lew Wallace had to face, a task that would have daunted Hercules.

The Santa Fe Ring was a group of lawyers and businessmen who used unscrupulous legal, political, and business tactics to acquire Spanish and Mexican land grants after the Mexican War (1846–1848). Thomas B. Catron and Stephen Elkins are reputed to have been two of the leaders of the Republican political machine that dominated territorial affairs from the late 1860s to the mid-1880s. The block of buildings facing the Plaza, on the east side, is known as the Catron Block. The building at 53 Old Santa Fe Trail, built in 1891, originally housed the Catron & Elkins law firm.

READ MORE ABOUT . . .

THE WILD WEST AND NEW MEXICO TERRITORY

♦ One of the best historical works is *The West of Billy, the Kid* (1998) by **Frederick W. Nolan**, who also wrote a new annotated version in 2000 of the original *Pat F. Garrett's Authentic Life of Billy, the Kid*, published in 1882.

♦ **Conrad Richter**'s *The Sea of Grass* is a 1936 epic novel based on the conflicts in the Lincoln County War and the life of one family over generations. The book was made into a 1947 motion picture by the same name, starring Spencer Tracy, Katharine Hepburn, and Melvyn Douglas. It is available for home viewing.

♦ **Harvey Fergusson**'s *Grant of Kingdom* (1950) covers some of the same ground as a fictionalized account of the life and times of Lucien Bonaparte Maxwell, who owned the largest piece of land in the territory at the time. Maxwell looms large both in New Mexico history and in its literature, with so many myths interpreted as fact.

♦ *My Life on the Frontier, 1864–1882,* by **Miguel A. Otero**, was published in 1935 (reprinted in 1987). Otero was the first Hispano to serve as territorial governor, with one of the longest tenures, 1897–1906. His second memoir is entitled *My Nine Years as Governor of the Territory of New Mexico.*

♦ *The Incredible Elfego Baca: Good Man, Bad Man of the Old West*, by **Howard Bryan** (1993), is a rousing account of one of New Mexico's most colorful and controversial figures. Legends about Elfego Baca and his "nine lives" arise from real historic events and the company he kept, including Billy the Kid and Pancho Villa.

(Cont'd on next page)

(The Wild West, cont'd)

- *No Life for a Lady* (1941) is **Agnes Morley Cleaveland**'s account of growing up on a ranch in a remote area of New Mexico, an excellent perspective from an authentic pioneer woman.

- *Meridian: A Novel of Kit Carson's West* (1987), by the late **Norman Zollinger**, who lived in Albuquerque, gives an honorable view of the legendary Christopher "Kit" Carson, another of those larger-than-life figures who has been widely written about and portrayed as both villain and hero.

- *Shane,* by **Jack Shaefer** (who lived in Santa Fe), was published in 1949 and has become strongly identified with the 1953 motion picture. *Shane* has been called one of the most powerful stories about the taming of the West, pitting cattlemen against home-steaders, where the law of the land belongs to the fastest on the draw. *Shane* is not about New Mexico, but its themes resonate here. Shaefer, a former journalist and author of many books, lived in New Mexico for more than thirty years until his death in 1991.

- **Evan Connell**, another Santa Fe author whose books are not about New Mexico, wrote an acclaimed account of a historic event in the West that has become mythic. Connell's *Son of the Morning Star: Custer and the Little Bighorn* was published in 1984 and translated into a TV series in 1991.

- **Hampton Sides'** *Blood and Thunder: An Epic of the American West* (2006) has been heralded as a sweeping view of America's west-ward expansion, with the figure of Kit Carson central to the book, embodying both the idealism and the savagery of the era.

The tales about Henry McCarty—aka Kid Antrim, aka Billy the Kid, aka William H. Bonney—are legendary and many are true. From all accounts, he was proficient with a gun as well as being hot tempered, but the number of people he killed has been exaggerated. He could be a charming lad, a ladies' man, and a rash young punk who managed to get himself killed by the age of 21—but his name lives on in infamy, as they say.

Billy openly threatened to kill Lew Wallace after, he claimed, the governor reneged on a deal to grant him clemency. (Elsewhere on this walk is a place where Billy was supposedly jailed. He was often in jails around the state, where the equivalent to "George Washington Slept Here" is "Billy the Kid Was in Jail Here.")

Billy was killed by lawman Pat Garrett in Fort Sumner, New Mexico, in July 1881. That was the same year that Lew Wallace resigned as governor and became the ambassador to the Ottoman Empire—a place that would surely be less Byzantine than New Mexico!

Entire publishing industries have been devoted to Billy the Kid and he still provides fodder for novelists and historians. The latest controversy, over exhuming bodies and doing DNA tests to determine whether or not it was really Billy that Pat Garrett shot, is described in **Jay Miller**'s book, ***Billy the Kid Rides Again: Digging for the Truth,*** published in 2005. Miller, a New Mexico native, lives in Santa Fe where he writes a political column for the *Santa Fe New Mexican*.

Palace Gift Shop

As you walk down Washington Street, alongside the Palace of the Governors, you will pass the **Palace Gift Shop (B1)**, which has an outstanding book section of Southwest literature.

Fray Angélico Chávez, one of New Mexico's native sons, left an impressive literary legacy.

FRAY ANGÉLICO CHÁVEZ HISTORY LIBRARY

PAUSE IN FRONT OF THE STATUE of Fray Angélico Chávez, outside of the **History Library (3)** building named in his honor.

Fray Angélico Chávez (1910–1996) is one of Santa Fe's most beloved authors yet his name is unfamiliar outside of New Mexico. His legacy looms large here not only for his body of work but also because he is a native son who earned the respect and affection of his neighbors and readers.

Angélico Chávez was born Manuel Chávez in Wagon Mound (east of Las Vegas, New Mexico) but came to live in Santa Fe about age sixteen. He became a Franciscan priest and was given the name

Angélico in the seminary because his love of painting reminded the rector of the Italian Fra Angelico. He also served in the army and became a prominent New Mexican historian and writer. He wrote twenty-four books but may be best remembered for his work in cataloging the archives of the Archdiocese of Santa Fe.

Born into the distinguished Chávez family, one of the founding families of New Mexico, Angélico and many of his siblings achieved prominent positions in the state (some as elected officials). This tradition continues with the younger generations of Chávezes. Fray Angélico's book ***Origins of New Mexico Families: A Genealogy of the Spanish Colonial Period*** has been released in a 1992 edition, with a foreword by his nephew Thomas Chávez, a scholar who was the director of the Palace of the Governors and the National Hispanic Cultural Center.

A particular favorite of Fray Angélico's books is ***My Penitente Land: Reflections on Spanish New Mexico***, published in 1974 and reprinted in 1996. This book is about much more than the Penitentes; it maps the Spanish soul (*anima hispánica*) of this land (*tierra*), with its echoes of Castile and the Holy Land.

The Fray Angélico Chávez History Library is part of the Palace of the Governors; the Photo Archives of the Palace are housed in the Library. Scholars and writers rely heavily on the resources available, but any visitor may use the services and gain a glimpse of historic documents. Public hours vary, so call for an appointment.

Among the treasured documents are copies of the 1610 epic poem by Villagrá, including an original copy; the notebooks and papers of anthropologist Adolph Bandelier; and thirty foreign-language translations of the novel *Ben Hur*.

The Photo Archives contain more than seven hundred and fifty thousand images in various formats, including the work of noted photographers like Jesse L. Nusbaum (1887–1975), T. Harmon Parkhurst (1883–1952), and Edward T. Curtis (1868–1952).

Before moving on, take a look at the buildings directly across the street from the Fray Angélico statue. Side by side are two good examples of the designated architectural forms that make up the official **Santa Fe Style**.

☙

Historic Preservation and Santa Fe Style

The Inn of the Anasazi, a highly rated "boutique" hotel, displays the classic design elements of the **Spanish Pueblo style**, combining the building techniques of the Pueblo peoples and the Spanish (often incorporating Moorish adaptations). It features flat-roofed, single- or multi-storied structures made of adobe bricks (primarily mud-and-straw mixture), with a mud-plastered exterior and thick rounded walls, often with supporting buttresses. Other features are roof beams known as *vigas* and alternating ceiling supports called *latillas. Portals* (simple porticos) were added with round posts, topped with carved wooden *corbels*. It is customary to paint residential windows and doorframes blue.

The Burrito Company's building is an example of the **Territorial style**, dating from the 1860s and using accent materials like hard-burned bricks that were not available in New Mexico Territory before the railroad (and wagon trains) arrived. It features flat- or pitched-roofed, single- or multi-storied structures, usually made of adobe bricks with a mud-plastered exterior, but the thick walls are straight rather than rounded. The style incorporates Greek Revival features with wooden doors and window frames. *Portals* have square posts with more classic lines and brick coping added to parapets at the roofline.

READ MORE ABOUT . . .

SANTA FE STYLE

+ Dennis, Landt, and Lisl Dennis. *Behind Adobe Walls: The Hidden Homes and Gardens of Santa Fe and Taos*. San Francisco: Chronicle Books, 1997.
+ Hammett, Jerilou, Kingsley Hammett, and Peter Scholz. *The Essence of Santa Fe: From a Way of Life to a Style*. Santa Fe: Ancient City Press (an imprint of Gibbs Smith, Publisher), 2005.
+ Mather, Christine, and Sharon Woods. *Santa Fe Style*. New York: Rizzoli, 1993.
+ Warren, Nancy Hunter. *New Mexico Style: A Sourcebook of Traditional Architectural Details*. Santa Fe: Museum of New Mexico Press, Expanded ed., 1995.
+ Wilson, Chris. *Facing Southwest: The Life and Houses of John Gaw Meem*. New York: W. W. Norton & Company, 2002.
+ ——. *The Myth of Santa Fe: Creation of a Modern Regional Tradition*. Albuquerque: University of New Mexico Press, 1997.

The historic building standards and design forms of Santa Fe Style were codified in 1957 in the most comprehensive and detailed architectural style ordinance in the United States at the time. The code was the culmination of adaptations in the look of Santa Fe's historic buildings that began in 1916 and continued for two decades.

The original intent of historic preservation was to promote Santa Fe's distinctive image and cultural history to attract tourism. That aim was aided by the writers and artists who began relocating to Santa Fe in the '20s and '30s. Some of them produced art and articles, mostly commissioned by the Atchison, Topeka, and Santa Fe Railway (AT&SF) that touted the City of Holy Faith to the rest of the world. Others, who did not want the rest of the world to discover "their" Santa Fe, got involved in historic preservation because they came to care deeply about the older cultures and indigenous arts that attracted them in the first place.

John Gaw Meem is the architect most identified with Santa Fe Style architecture, although he did not invent it. He came to Santa Fe in 1920, seeking treatment for tuberculosis; he decided to make it his home, and left an impressive legacy of Meem-designed buildings. (A John Gaw Meem "masterpiece" home was on the market in Santa Fe for $15 million in 2002.)

Meem joined with authors **Mary Austin** and **Witter Bynner**, among others, to form the Old Santa Fe Association in 1926. (These authors are part of the Canyon Road Walk.) The organization has an active role today in overseeing the city's historic design enforcement, along with the Historic Santa Fe Foundation.

PRINCE AND SENA PLAZAS

HEAD BACK TO PALACE AVENUE, cross the street and turn left. As you near the end of the block, you will be facing **Prince and Sena Plazas (4)**, which appear to be one long building. **Prince Plaza**, the part of the structure with turquoise blue wooden posts, was the home of **L. Bradford Prince** (1840–1922), New Mexico territorial governor from 1889 until 1893. He resided here before, during, and after his tenure as governor—as the Palace of the Governors had to undergo repairs before he could move in.

Attorney, author, and politician, Prince was a resident of New York City, where he helped break the power of Tammany Hall, before he moved to New Mexico Territory in 1879 to become chief justice of its supreme court and, later, its governor.

A champion of preservation of history in all its forms, Prince was one of the first to advocate restoration of the decrepit Palace of the

Sena Plaza, the historic residence of generations of the Sena family, is now a retail center, with shops and restaurants. The famous Villagra Book Shop moved here in 1927, remaining for more than fifty years.

Governors instead of demolition, as some were proposing. He read history, became active in the Historical Society of New Mexico, and worked tirelessly for the preservation of Spanish colonial mission churches. His book on **Spanish Mission Churches of New Mexico** was published in 1915.

109 East Palace

The doorway of **109 East Palace** (leading into the Onorato shop) has its story to tell: through that door passed many of the greatest scientists of the twentieth century when they arrived to work on the Manhattan Project in 1943. A woman named Dorothy McKibben was hired by J. Robert Oppenheimer to run the Santa Fe office of the secret weapons laboratory at Los Alamos. Here, in a disguised storefront operation, she greeted newly arrived scientists, reminding them to use their aliases while in town and never to identify themselves as physicists. They entered the front door, had papers processed, and left by the back door—not knowing that they faced a forty-mile trip over rugged terrain to reach the top-secret community that would be their home for several years.

109 East Palace: Robert Oppenheimer and the Secret City of Los Alamos, by **Jennet Conant**, was one of several excellent books published in 2005 about Oppenheimer and the Manhattan Project. "Less about the science of building the bomb, the book highlights the creation of a unique place and time in which that bomb could be built, and Conant (the granddaughter of a Manhattan Project administrator) brings to life the colorful eccentric town of thousands that sprang up on a New Mexico mesa and achieved the unthinkable," said *Publisher's Weekly*.

Another popular book on the era is *The House at Otowi Bridge: The Story of Edith Warner and Los Alamos*, by **Peggy Pond Church**, published in 1959. It is a delightful story of a particular time in our history and also one that illustrates a paradox about New Mexico and Santa Fe. This is a place of striking contrasts: affluence lives side by side with dire poverty as quantum physics and chaos theory coexist with ancient tribal ways. Sophisticated and privileged people gravitate to the capital city's cultural richness and natural beauty, while the children of long-time residents drop out of high school at alarming rates and have to leave town to find jobs.

Our literature reflects these extremes. The true story of Edith Warner is a case in point. Warner, who had come here for rest and restoration, found herself "taking root" in a little house situated near the Otowi Crossing of the Rio Grande, between Los Alamos and the San Ildefonso Pueblo. As she and the Pueblo peoples became more acquainted, the rhythms of her new life expanded to include personal relationships with the scientists of the Manhattan Project. They came to her tearoom for good food, conversation, and a respite from intense pressures. Many of Edith Warner's Christmas letters are reproduced in the book, adding to the firsthand experience of her story.

> *The climax came on that August day when the report of the atomic bomb flashed around the world. It seemed fitting that it was Kitty Oppenheimer who, coming for vegetables, brought the news. I had not known what was being done up there, though in the beginning I had suspected atomic research. Much was now explained. Now I can tell you that Conant and Compton came in through the kitchen door to eat ragout and chocolate cake; that Fermi, Allison, Teller, Parsons came many times; that Oppenheimer was the man I knew in pre-war years and who made it possible for the Hill people to come down. . . . It has been an incredible experience for a woman who chose to live in a supposedly isolated spot. In no other place could I have had the privilege of knowing Niels Bohr, who is not only a great scientist but a great man. In no other way could I have seen develop a group feeling of responsibility for presenting the facts to the people and urging the only wise course—international control of atomic energy and bombs.*

> Excerpt from Edith Warner's 1945 Christmas letter, in
> *The House at Otowi Bridge: The Story of Edith Warner and Los Alamos* (1959)
> by Peggy Pond Church

At the house at Otowi Bridge, two vastly different worlds came together in harmony, if only for a while—the ancient and earthbound with the modern and technology-proud, each with strong spiritual elements. This phenomenon is quintessential New Mexico. The book is a classic and not to be missed.

Sena Plaza

The portion of the long building with brown posts is the historic residence of the Sena family, one of Santa Fe's oldest families. The land that the house sits on had been in the family since 1844, and the early part of the house was built by 1864. Over the years, the house grew, as did generations of Senas. It is built of adobe brick with an interior *placita*, or patio. In 1927, the Sena heirs sold the house, which was then restored. Today it houses shops and restaurants.

Villagra Book Shop

Santa Fe's first bookstore, the **Villagra Book Shop** (named for the conquistador poet) was located in **Sena Plaza**, in the spot that today houses Gusterman Silversmiths. The bookstore began in 1921 when **Roberta Robey** garnered a corner of a stationery store on the Plaza, across from La Fonda Hotel, to sell books. Prior to that, few books were sold in Santa Fe except occasional selections at curio shops, but a small lending library existed, **Willard "Spud" Johnson** recalled in a 1963 article in the *Santa Fe New Mexican*'s *Pasatiempo* (more about Johnson on the Canyon Road Walk).

Robey moved the growing business to historic Sena Plaza in 1927, where it became one of Santa Fe's favorite spots for the literati—and for anyone wanting a good story from a book or by word of mouth. Browsers frequently occupied an armchair by the corner fireplace and Johnson is sure that **Willa Cather** sat there on one occasion.

The Villagra Book Shop maintained a tradition of daily "tea" during this time, featuring *mitote* (gossip) and martinis, the latter delivered promptly at 4:00 p.m. from the nearby La Fonda Hotel.

Robey ventured into publishing when the first Villagra Book Shop book was published in 1933. The bookshop changed hands in 1936 when she sold it, but several owners kept it going until the early 1960s when **Nancy Lane** took it over.

By that time, **Ancient City Book Shop**, a small bookstore selling out-of-print titles and Southwest paperbacks, had opened nearby in Sena Plaza. Ancient City proprietor **Robert Kadlec** began his first publishing project in 1961, producing **La Casa Adobe**, by New Mexican architect **William Lumpkins** (1909–2000), and **Ancient City Press** was born.

Kadlec and his bookseller-neighbor Lane decided to partner in a new version of the old Villagra tradition and, in the early '60s, began to offer midafternoon Eskimo Pies to locals who regularly stopped by to enjoy these occasions, **Marta Weigle** recalls. ("The Folklorist as Publisher," a paper delivered by Weigle to the American Folklore Society in 1989.)

The Villagra Book Shop lived on with several more changes in ownership until it closed in the early 1980s.

Nicholas Potter Bookseller

Just up the street at 211 East Palace is **Nicholas Potter Bookseller (B2)**, Santa Fe's oldest bookstore for used and collectible books. Potter is a second-generation Santa Fe bookseller dealing in general used and out-of-print books, including a good selection of Southwest literature.

MUSEUM OF THE INSTITUTE OF AMERICAN INDIAN ARTS

OPPOSITE THE CATHEDRAL is the **Museum of the Institute of American Indian Arts (5)**, which showcases contemporary Native American Fine Art. The museum is part of the Institute of American Indian Arts (IAIA), a four-year fine arts college offering degrees in creative writing, studio arts, visual communications, and museum studies. Founded in 1962, the IAIA is a multitribal center of higher education dedicated to the preservation, study, and contemporary expression of

American Indian and Alaska Native arts and cultures. The museum has been in this building, the former Santa Fe post office, since 1991. The campus of IAIA is south of town.

N. Scott Momaday, one of the most acclaimed Native American writers, lives at the Jemez Pueblo, northwest of Santa Fe. He serves on the board of many Santa Fe organizations, and he is part of the IAIA adjunct faculty in its Center of Arts and Cultural Studies.

Momaday, a Pulitzer Prize–winning author, is a Kiowa who was born in Oklahoma but grew up at the Jemez Pueblo where his parents were teachers. Painting and writing came naturally to him; his father was a painter and master storyteller and his mother was a writer. Momaday has illustrated many of his books; his art has been exhibited in the United States and abroad, including a one-man, twenty-year retrospective at the Wheelwright Museum in Santa Fe.

N. Scott Momaday, PhD, is one of the leading authorities on the oral tradition of native peoples. Having grown up with family and tribal stories, he has devoted much of his life to safeguarding this oral tradition and other aspects of native culture, developing courses and curricula at several universities.

Many would recognize him from his appearances in the PBS documentary series *The West* (1996) and other television and film work. Although Momaday is best known for the novel ***House Made of Dawn***, which won the Pulitzer Prize for Fiction in 1969, he has written in all genres, including poetry and drama.

House Made of Dawn is the story of a Jemez Pueblo man and his difficult adjustment after World War II to the duality in his life—one foot in the Pueblo realm and the other in the white man's world.

Other important books by Momaday are *The Ancient Child* (1989), *The Way to Rainy Mountain* (1969), and *The Names: A Memoir* (1976).

The Cathedral Basilica of St. Francis of Assisi, one of Santa Fe's most prominent landmarks, is identified with the award-winning novel Death Comes for the Archbishop.

CATHEDRAL BASILICA
OF ST. FRANCIS OF ASSISI

BEFORE CROSSING THE STREET to the **Cathedral Basilica of St. Francis of Assisi (6)**, pause at the corner, facing it, to get a full view of this prominent Santa Fe landmark, identified with the best-known novel about Santa Fe, ***Death Comes for the Archbishop***, by **Willa Cather**. The Cathedral Basilica of St. Francis of Assisi is the mother church of the Archdiocese of Santa Fe. It could not have been built in its Romanesque style on its present site if the city's 1957 historic building design codes had been in force in 1869 when the cornerstone was laid. (Today's historic building ordinance allows only Spanish Pueblo and Territorial styles in Santa Fe's historic districts.)

The cathedral was built by French-born archbishop **Jean Baptiste Lamy** between 1869 and 1886. He had been sent by the Vatican to New Mexico Territory to make reforms in local parish practices and to restore ecclesiastical standards. He was the first Catholic bishop (later archbishop) to reside in Santa Fe. Lamy is buried in a crypt behind the altar in the cathedral.

Here is the Santa Fe of 1851, first glimpsed by the Lamy-inspired character after a long and arduous journey, in the 1927 award-winning novel, *Death Comes for the Archbishop*:

> Father Latour could distinguish low brown shapes, like earthworks, lying at the base of wrinkled green mountains with bare tops . . . as the wagons went forward and the sun sank lower, a sweep of red carnelian-coloured hills lying at the foot of the mountains came into view; they curved like two arms about a depression in the plain; and in that depression was Santa Fé, at last! A thin, wavering adobe town . . . a green plaza . . . at one end a church with two earthen towers that rose high above the flatness . . . the church towers, and all the low adobe houses, were rose colour in that light.

In fact, the real-life Lamy, arriving in 1851, had a large influence on the look of the town. In addition to the Romanesque cathedral, he was also responsible for the Gothic Revival Loretto Chapel, St. Vincent's Hospital, and the original St. Michael's College. Stone masonry, European artisans, and building styles were used in all of these downtown structures that still exist in one form or another.

Lamy's legacy is interpreted in contrasting ways by residents of Santa Fe and *el norte* (generally referring to the towns and villages north of Santa Fe, extending all the way to present-day Colorado). To some, he brought needed changes to the Catholic Church in New Mexico, and is regarded as a savior of sorts who founded schools and helped to improve living conditions in a neglected region. To others, he was a "foreign" tyrant who never tried to understand or appreciate local Hispanic culture and tradition, replaced native clergy with Europeans, and wielded power unfairly.

The controversy surrounding Lamy is reflected in how New Mexicans regard Willa Cather's novel. Some admire it as an elegant and authentic picture of people and events; others reject it as a biased account that identifies entirely with the archbishop character and gives short shrift to the accomplishments of local leaders such as Padre Martínez of Taos, who was excommunicated by the real-life Lamy.

Cather's friend **Mary Austin**, the writer in whose Santa Fe home Cather stayed while writing portions of the novel, was unhappy with the book. Austin felt that Cather had gone overboard in presenting Lamy's European vision of what Santa Fe should be. Cather, a distinguished writer who grew up in Nebraska and lived in New York for many years, had visited Santa Fe often. She decided to write a book about the history of the Southwest through the lens of the Catholic Church, selecting Lamy as the symbol of positive reformation in the City of Holy Faith.

ଔ
Controversy and Reform

To better understand the context of this controversy, recall that Spain had deliberately kept its colonies isolated from all outside influences. This meant that the Catholics in Santa Fe and *el norte* were largely underserved because of the small number of overworked Franciscan priests and missionaries—and the nearest Catholic bishop resided many miles away in Durango, Mexico.

After 1821, when this territory became part of the Mexican Republic, Spain recalled its clergy, and New Mexico was left with even fewer priests and missionaries to serve its people. Those who remained had great territories to support with few resources. Itinerant priests would travel to the remote villages, but in the interim, couples might be living as man and wife, waiting to have their vows sanctified.

Lay clergy, priests with partial seminary training, and a few legitimate clergy were said to be using their offices for personal gain, fathering children, and involving themselves in local politics.

The Penitente Brothers (*los hermanos*) became prominent in colonial New Mexico during this time, the late eighteenth and early nineteenth centuries. The chronic shortage of Catholic clergy in the region left a void that the Brothers tried to fill. Although the Penitentes are best known for their secret rituals and acts of penance during Holy Week, they also performed religious functions in the absence of clergy, such as burials, and served as an informal mutual aid society, with women also playing a role.

The Penitentes were "outlawed" by Lamy, who said that the church would provide more priests and ordered the *Hermanos* to end their secret fraternity. Penitentes still exist proudly and openly today in New Mexico. A beautiful book on this subject is ***En Divina Luz: The Penitente Moradas of New Mexico***, published in 1994, with text by Michael Wallis and photographs by Craig Varjabedian.

The Vatican had ordered Lamy to go to the New Mexico Territory to restore order, weed out corruption, and uphold Catholic doctrine and practices. Sound familiar? That is close to the mission that was handed to Territorial Governor Lew Wallace in 1878 (discussed earlier in this walk), but Lamy arrived in 1851. By the time Wallace came here, almost thirty years later, New Mexico was still in need of "civilizing," lacking law and order, although the Catholic Church had been strengthened.

Returning to the literary discussion, I recommend reading *Death Comes for the Archbishop,* along with two other books that map much of the same terrain and offer balancing perspectives. These are Paul Horgan's **Lamy of Santa Fe: His Life and Times** (1975), and **But Time and Chance: The Story of Padre Martínez of Taos, 1793–1867**, published in 1981 by Fray Angélico Chávez.

Horgan's biography of Lamy won the Pulitzer Prize for History and is a well-documented account, based on extended research, partly in the Vatican library in Rome. Fray Angélico's biography of **Padre Antonio José Martínez** is also well researched, given Chávez's historian's instincts and his access to the archives of the Archdiocese of Santa Fe. While Cather's novel follows the historical events of Lamy's life and the unfolding events after his arrival, both of the biographies present the actual history, and the two views add perspective to understanding a turbulent time in New Mexico.

Padre Martínez and author Paul Horgan deserve a few more words at this juncture.

A portrait of Martínez in the Palace of the Governors is New Mexico's earliest known daguerreotype (date unknown). This image is the one most often identified with Padre Martínez, with the famous "scowl" indicating a severity that was likely unintended. The text underneath the portrait briefly describes his significance in New Mexico's history: *"Padre Antonio José Martínez (1793–1867), Catholic priest, philosopher, educator, printer, and revolutionary, he played key roles in the transition of Northern New Mexico from Republican*

Mexico to U.S. Territory. He was an outspoken champion of New Mexico's traditional Roman Catholic practices and his resistance to the European influence of the new Bishop Jean Baptiste Lamy, from 1850 on, led Lamy to excommunicate him."

Padre Martínez was mentioned earlier in this walk as having printed the first book in New Mexico in 1835, a spelling primer.

Paul Horgan (1903–1995) came to New Mexico as a boy from Buffalo, New York. He attended high school in Albuquerque, where he became friends with the Fergusson family whose literary contributions to New Mexico are significant (more about them later in the walk). Horgan attended the New Mexico Military Institute (NMMI) in Roswell, and later served as its librarian. He and Peter Hurd, who became famous for his art, were fellow students at NMMI and lifelong friends.

Horgan became acquainted with **Witter Bynner** and many of the writers and artists in Santa Fe and Taos in the '30s and '40s. After moving east, he spent summers in Santa Fe until a heart condition precluded his spending time at this altitude. In later life, he was professor emeritus and writer-in-residence at Wesleyan University in Middletown, Connecticut, where he died.

Horgan twice earned the Pulitzer Prize for History for ***Great River: The Story of the Rio Grande in North American History***, published in 1954, and for the Lamy biography. A prolific writer in many genres, he also dabbled in painting and provided illustrations for some of his books. Other noteworthy Horgan books are ***The Habit of Empire*** (nonfiction, 1938), and ***The Centuries of Santa Fe*** (nonfiction with fictional vignettes, 1956). ***A Distant Trumpet***, a historical novel published in 1960, was made into a motion picture by the same name in 1964, starring Troy Donahue.

A 1920s parade of covered wagons outside of La Fonda depicts an earlier time when traders from the Santa Fe Trail sought lodging at the Inn at the End of the Trail.

LA FONDA HOTEL

ENTER THE HISTORIC **La Fonda Hotel (7)** through the San Francisco Street entrance and find a seat in a back corner alcove at the foot of the stairway (rear left, off the main lobby, as you enter). This is a good place to rest and later, perhaps, to browse at the **La Fonda Newsstand (B3)**.

La Fonda Newsstand
Located in the hotel lobby, the **La Fonda Newsstand (B3)** has an excellent selection of Southwest literature.

La Fonda (the inn) is the *grande dame* of Santa Fe's hotels, with a history to match its long-standing dominance of the local social and cultural scene. Records indicate some kind of inn or lodgings at the end of the Santa Fe Trail when it opened in 1821. Other records show an inn of some sort among the earliest businesses built on the Santa Fe Plaza from its inception. Early in the territorial days, about 1848, a hotel in the same location was called the U.S. Hotel and later became known as the Exchange Hotel—and that name lasted for nearly sixty years.

By the time New Mexico became a state in 1912, the Exchange Hotel had become so deteriorated that it was torn down in 1919, making way for a new hotel financed by citizen investors through a World War I bond rally. That hotel, built in 1920 on the same site, was later acquired by AT&SF railroad, which leased it to Fred

Indian Detours, begun in 1926 by Fred Harvey, operated out of La Fonda, taking visitors to the Indian Pueblos in touring cars (Harveycars) for $50 per person. The tours attracted affluent visitors from the East.

Harvey in 1926. It became one of the famous **Harvey Houses** until 1969. In its present incarnation, La Fonda is essentially the same building as that Harvey House, although it has experienced several renovations and additions.

Lesley Poling Kempes, who lives in Abiquiú, where Georgia O'Keeffe lived, wrote *The Harvey Girls: Women Who Opened the West* (1991), which offers entertaining insights into this colorful period when tourism was becoming a major industry in the Southwest.

Another New Mexican, **Victoria E. Dye**, who worked in New Mexico's tourism sector, has written about this phenomenon in *All Aboard for Santa Fe: Railway Promotion of the Southwest, 1890s to 1930s* (2005).

"The La Fonda," as the locals call it, has been the place to see and be seen for most of its years. Visiting dignitaries from times past and present who stayed here include **General and Mrs. Ulysses S. Grant**, **President and Mrs. Rutherford B. Hayes**, **Charles Lindbergh**, **Thornton Wilder**, and **Henry and Clare Boothe Luce**. Film stars on location who have signed the guest register include **James Stewart**, **Errol Flynn**, **Greer Garson**, **Robert Duvall**, **Diane Keaton**, and **John Travolta**.

This hotel was the scene of the annual masquerade ball during the '30s and '40s when

B. B. (Brian Boru) Dunne, in his signature hat, was a "fixture" at La Fonda hotel, the best spot to pick up news for his New Mexican *column on Santa Fe society.*

the Bohemian writers and artists dominated the Santa Fe social scene. One of Santa Fe's resident "eccentrics" used to hang out in the La Fonda lobby, looking for gossipy tidbits to report in his society column for the local newspaper. He was **B.B. (Brian Boru) Dunne**; his portrait still hangs in the lobby.

The late **Richard Bradford**, author of the beloved coming-of-age story ***Red Sky at Morning*** (1968), recalled Dunne and his signature hat in an interview with **John Pen La Farge**, Santa Fe author and historian, who is the son of the late Pulitzer Prize–winning author **Oliver La Farge**.

> *And he had a famous hat, flat-topped, very broad brimmed brown hat—not quite a cowboy hat, more like a southern-planter hat with a concha belt around the crown.*
>
> *Very famous hat, wore it all the time. I assume he wore it to bed and in the bath; I don't know, . . . And over the years, apparently, a thousand people had asked B.B. that if, God forbid, he should ever die, would he please bequeath his hat to that person. A thousand people had asked him, he'd agreed a thousand times. When he did die, a thousand people turned up at his house on the corner of Garcia and Acequia Madre, clamoring, looking for the lawyers, demanding immediate probate so they could get his hat. I don't know what happened to his hat, finally. It may have been buried with him.*
>
> —Richard Bradford,
> excerpt from *Turn Left at the Sleeping Dog* (2001)
> by John Pen La Farge

The woman known as New Mexico's First Lady of Letters, **Erna Fergusson** (1888–1964), also has a connection to La Fonda Hotel. Early in the Harvey House years, she was hired by Fred Harvey to organize and manage the **Indian Detours** company operated out of La Fonda. Indian Detours ("Detourism" it has been called) began in 1926, taking visitors (for $50 per person) out to the pueblos in touring cars (Harveycars) with trained escorts (couriers) to experience native culture and arts firsthand.

Erna Fergusson, born into a distinguished Albuquerque pioneer family, has been called New Mexico's First Lady of Letters. New Mexico: A Pageant of Three Peoples *is one of her most popular books.*

Fergusson, who was a former teacher, had been writing for the *Albuquerque Herald* and had also formed her own company, Koshare Tours, with a woman colleague. Because she was always welcome at the pueblos, having shown the proper respect and forming lasting relationships, Erna Fergusson was the ideal person to train the young women who were employed as couriers for Indian Detours. She was in the "dude wrangling business," as she called it.

Erna Fergusson was born into a distinguished Albuquerque family, and apart from travels and time spent away for education, she lived most of her life there. (A branch of the Albuquerque Public Library is named in her honor.) She was a frequent visitor to Santa Fe, became part of the writers and artists group, and lived here for a while during her employment with the Indian Detours.

Among **Erna Fergusson**'s books, ***Dancing Gods*** (1931), about Indian ceremonial dances, and ***New Mexico: A Pageant of Three Peoples*** (1951, reprinted 1964) are still regarded as significant contributions to Southwest literature.

Her grandfather was Franz Huning, a German emigrant who had come to New Mexico over the Santa Fe Trail in 1853, later bringing his young bride to the settlement on the Rio Grande at Albuquerque. He helped develop the area and became quite prosperous, especially after the coming of the railroad.

Erna's father, Harvey Fergusson, arrived in Albuquerque in 1882 to practice law; later, he represented New Mexico as a territory and, after statehood, in Congress in Washington, D.C.

Harvey Fergusson (1890–1971) is also the name of Erna's younger brother who had a successful literary career. He visited Santa Fe often but never lived here, spending most of his life in Albuquerque and California. Among Harvey's books about New Mexico, ***The Conquest of Don Pedro*** (1954), ***Grant of Kingdom*** (1950), and ***Wolf Song*** (1927) are highly recommended. In ***Footloose McGarnigal*** (1930), Harvey wrote a novel satirizing the Anglo artists of Santa Fe and Taos in the late 1920s who "worshipped the primitive." Along with some humorous jabs at particular people that he knew, Fergusson offers some serious insights into the era, largely from an outsider's point-of-view.

BURRO ALLEY

LEAVING LA FONDA, turn left on San Francisco Street and go two blocks to Galisteo Street; turn right to cross San Francisco Street. You will see Burro Alley just ahead on the right. **Burro Alley (8)** was a center of travel and trade during the early territorial days—and the "red light district" of Santa Fe at the time. Though only one block long today, this tiny byway was a thriving thoroughfare in the early 1800s, with a mix of businesses and residences side by side, many of the old adobe buildings sharing common walls. The sculpture of the burro carrying a bundle of firewood depicts the major activity on this little street after the turn of the century. Vendors of firewood would bring their loads down from the mountains on the burros and sell them on what became known as Burro Alley.

One of this district's best known citizens during those bawdy territorial days was **La Doña Tules**, whose real name was Gertrudis Barcelo. She was the proprietress of the largest gambling

Burro Alley (ca. 1880–1885) during New Mexico's wild territorial days was a center for trade, gambling, and other forms of entertainment.

house on the street and a famous monte dealer (a popular card game of chance). She had earned a reputation for being a shrewd businesswoman and a vivacious lady of questionable virtue. Yes, she was surely a madam, with the proverbial heart of gold, who longed for respectability.

All of the powerful men in Santa Fe patronized her *sala* (gambling house and saloon), along with the American traders, trappers, mountain men, and others who came to take part in the commerce made possible by the Santa Fe Trail. She had money enough to lend to the Army when its payroll was held up on the trail, and in return for the favor, she requested and received a military escort to the Victory Ball, where she danced among the elite of Santa Fe.

Doña Tules saved a large sum of money to pay for a funeral fit for a queen, and when she died in 1852 (about the age of fifty-two), she went out in grand style. It is said that most of the respectable ladies who shunned her in life were made to attend her funeral by their husbands. La Tules would have liked that.

Several stories about Doña Tules have become legend, and a novel based on her life tells them all. ***The Wind Leaves No Shadow***, written by **Ruth Laughlin** (previously Ruth Laughlin Barker), was published in 1948 (reprints 1951, 1992). The respected author Oliver La Farge pronounced it "a book to be read with excitement and delight . . . a tale inherently loaded with incident and suspense . . . an innately gorgeous story, excellently told."

Collected Works Bookstore

Across the street from Burro Alley is **Collected Works Bookstore (B4)**, 208B West San Francisco Street, a Santa Fe institution since 1978. This independent bookstore specializes in books about New Mexico and the Southwest, presenting many renowned local and national authors to read from their works. On a bronze plaque on the outside wall near the bookstore entrance (to the right of the doorway) is one of many "Billy, the Kid was in jail here" inscriptions found in places around New Mexico.

LENSIC THEATER

TURN AROUND AND LOOK at the **Lensic Theater (9)** on West San Francisco Street, opposite the bookstore and left of Burro Alley. The Lensic Performing Arts Center rose like a phoenix from the shell of the old Lensic Theater, reopening in 2001 after extensive restoration

Rita Hayworth, Roy Rogers, and Judy Garland are among the Hollywood stars who have performed on stage at the Lensic Theater, built in 1931. The Trapp Family Singers and Yehudi Menuhin also appeared. Today, it is the leading downtown venue for Santa Fe's performing arts.

and reconstruction. It is Santa Fe's premier venue for the performing arts, apart from the Santa Fe Opera House. Music of all kinds, vintage films, lectures, and readings by leading authors from around the world, troupes of acrobats, and dance programs (traditional to contemporary)—all are presented at the Lensic.

Built in 1931 as one of the wonderful old movie houses with elaborate Moorish-Spanish architecture and old-world décor, the Lensic Theater was still functioning, barely, as a movie house until 1999. In its heyday, it hosted the world premiere of the 1941 motion picture **Santa Fe Trail**, starring **Errol Flynn**, **Olivia de Havilland**, and **Ronald Reagan** (as George Armstrong Custer). The movie was not filmed in New Mexico, and its script took liberties with the history implied in its title, but Santa Fe and its local glitterati welcomed the cast with great fanfare. Today, the Lensic is the primary venue for the respected *Readings and Conversations* author series presented by the Santa Fe–based **Lannan Foundation**.

Turn around and head towards the Cathedral on San Francisco Street. Walk up to Don Gaspar Street, about one and one-half blocks, and turn right. You are going to the **River Walk** along the Alameda, two blocks away. You will pass **Café Pasqual's** on the left at the intersection of Don Gaspar and Water Streets. This is one of the most popular places in town for breakfast or brunch—well worth the wait for a table. Highly regarded owner-chef Katherine Kagel prepares all recipes with organic or natural ingredients. If you wish to sit at the community table, the wait in line will be shorter—and you never know whom you might meet. The employees call the community table at Pasqual's the Love Boat because at least two marriages have resulted from people who met there.

On the right as you cross Water Street is the **Hotel St. Francis**, one of the few places in Santa Fe to provide a "proper" English tea service.

Stay to the left on Don Gaspar as you approach Alameda Street and you will see an art gallery display of outdoor sculpture—just another example of the range of art to be found in Santa Fe, one of the country's largest art markets.

SANTA FE RIVER WALK

CROSS ALAMEDA STREET and you will find yourself on the footpath of the **Santa Fe River Walk (10)**, along the Alameda. Listen carefully and you may hear **La Llorona** (the Wailing Woman) who is a universal figure throughout the Spanish-speaking world:

> *The stories regarding this popular folkloric figure abound and may well differ from one village to another. One common version is that the Wailing Woman, in a moment of uncontrolled rage, drowned her two children by the river and now roams its banks in search of them. The punishment for her crime is to hear her children's voices every time she walks along the river.*

> —Nasario García,
> local author and folklorist,
> excerpt from *Brujas, Bultos, y Brasas:
> Tales of Witchcraft and the Supernatural in the Pecos Valley* (1999)

Another aspect of the La Llorona legend is her usefulness in "scaring" youngsters into obedience. Many Santa Feans say that they grew up afraid of La Llorona, generally believed to be a ghost or banshee-like wraith. Mothers warn their small children that the Wailing Woman might come for them if they do not behave.

As you walk the two blocks to Old Santa Fe Trail, pause at the corner of the Trail and Alameda Street and observe the magnificent **Inn at Loretto**, probably the most photographed site in downtown Santa Fe—especially at Christmas. It is an excellent example of Spanish Pueblo architecture.

THE LORETTO CHAPEL

TURN LEFT ON THE OLD SANTA FE TRAIL to arrive at the **Loretto Chapel (11),** next door to the Inn at Loretto. The chapel is the home of the famous "Miraculous Staircase" and operates as a private non-denominational chapel for weddings and events.

Built in the 1870s, it is said to be the first Gothic structure west of the Mississippi River, complete with spires, buttresses, and stained-glass windows imported from France. The Chapel of Our Lady of Light served the Loretto Academy, a girls' school operated by the Sisters of Loretto, until the late 1960s.

The legendary story of the Miraculous Staircase involves, if not a miracle, at least two mysteries: the identity of its creator and the physics of its construction. As the chapel neared completion, the lack of access to the choir loft posed a great problem for the Sisters. Using a ladder to reach the choir loft was ruled out, and there was no room for a standard staircase.

Seeking divine guidance, the Sisters made a Novena to their patron saint, St. Joseph the Carpenter. As legend has it, on the ninth and final day, an unknown carpenter arrived to design and construct a circular staircase to the choir loft. The only tools he brought were a saw, carpenter's square, hammer, and tubs for soaking the wood.

The completed staircase contains thirty-three steps in two full 360-degree turns—with no center support or side support. When the staircase was finished, the carpenter disappeared without seeking payment. The Sisters believed that he was St. Joseph, come to answer their prayers.

To learn more, read *Loretto: The Sisters and Their Santa Fe Chapel* (2002), by Santa Fe author Mary Straw Cook.

This is the last stop on the Downtown Santa Fe Walk. Follow Old Santa Fe Trail another block or so to get back to the Plaza.

The legendary story of the Miraculous Staircase of the Loretto Chapel involves, if not a miracle, at least two mysteries.

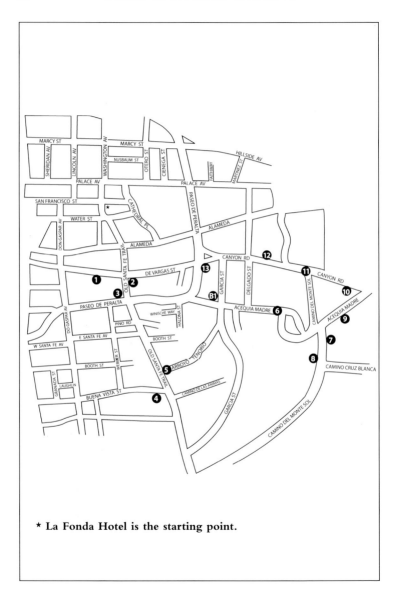

★ La Fonda Hotel is the starting point.

OLD SANTA FE TRAIL TO CANYON ROAD

☙

1 Barrio de Analco

2 San Miguel Mission Chapel

3 New Mexico Capitol

4 Witter Bynner's Home
(Inn of the Turquoise Bear)

5 Arroyo Tenorio to
Acequia Madre

   B1 *Garcia Street Books* and
   Downtown Subscription

6 Acequia Madre to
Camino del Monte Sol

7 Mary Austin's Home
(Chiaroscuro
Contemporary Art)

8 Will Shuster's Home

9 Acequia Madre and
Don Miguel

10 Gerald Cassidy Placita

11 Canyon Road

12 El Zaguán

13 Adolph Bandelier's Home
(Sherwood's Spirit of America
Gallery)

OLD SANTA FE TRAIL
TO CANYON ROAD

Start at La Fonda Hotel and follow the Old Santa Fe Trail south, away from the Plaza. At the end of the block, cross to Shelby Street and continue for one block to Alameda Street. Cross Alameda and go over the old Santa Fe River footbridge, turning right for a short distance before you arrive at a gate. Go left into the gate and you will be in a parking area behind the building of the New Mexico Supreme Court. Ascend the mild slope to East de Vargas Street and turn left.

BARRIO DE ANALCO

YOU ARE NOW in the **Barrio de Analco (1)**, one of the oldest neighborhoods in the nation, dating from the early 1600s. It was the home of the **Tlaxcalan Indians** who came with the Spanish to settle Santa Fe. *Analco* is the Nahuatl word for "the other side of the water." This neighborhood is across the river from the Plaza, where the Spanish built their homes.

The Tlaxcalans were enemies of the Aztecs and had joined with the Spanish in defeating them. Those who came north to a new life were treated as a servant class and lived apart from the Spanish, as required by Spanish law at the time. This quarter was the Indians' home, and the San Miguel Church was built for (and by) them. (These Tlaxcalans had adopted the Spanish religion.)

The old mission church at the end of the street is all that remains from that era. The *barrio* (neighborhood or district) was razed during the Pueblo Revolt of 1680, with the residents escaping to the Palace of the Governors for refuge. They fled Santa Fe with the Spanish. After the reconquest in 1693, only a few of the original settlers returned, but the barrio was rebuilt and became home to Spanish soldiers and their families. A plaque near the corner of East de Vargas and Old Santa Fe Trail briefly describes this history.

Many of the historic homes here date from the early to mid-eighteenth century, with bronze plaques designating them worthy of preservation by the **Historic Santa Fe Foundation** (founded in 1961). Several of these houses on East De Vargas have been purchased by the foundation and are private residences.

The **Santa Fe Playhouse**, on the right, is the community theater where the annual Fiesta Melodrama is presented along with other productions. Santa Fe writers and artists participate in producing the melodrama each year, a parody of local issues and personalities. This tradition dates back to 1919 when the writer **Mary Austin** founded the **Community Theater of Santa Fe**. Many of the writers and artists living in Santa Fe in the '20s and '30s were involved in the local drama productions. The Santa Fe Players, as they came to be known, wrote, performed, painted scenery, designed sets—and generally had a grand time. We will be meeting many of them on this walk.

The Barrio de Analco extends along East de Vargas Street to the Paseo de Peralta, including the **Oldest House**, east of the Upper Crust pizzeria. It is perhaps the oldest surviving house in Santa Fe, believed to date from 1740–1760, but certainly not the oldest in the nation, as is often claimed.

SAN MIGUEL MISSION CHAPEL

ONE OF THE OLDEST CHURCHES in the United States, **San Miguel Mission Chapel (2)** is still in use. The simple adobe structure was built circa 1610 in the New Mexico Mission style by the Tlaxcalan Indians of Mexico. The San Miguel Mission became their parish church.

The church was badly damaged in the 1680 Pueblo Revolt but was restored and enlarged in 1710. On display in the chapel are

The San Miguel Mission, at the corner of DeVargas Street and Old Santa Fe Trail, is all that survives from the early 1610 settlement in the Barrio de Analco, one of the oldest neighborhoods in the nation.

priceless statues and rare paintings on buffalo hides—and the San José Bell, believed to have been cast in Spain in 1356, weighing nearly eight hundred pounds.

In the nineteenth century, the Christian Brothers arrived in Santa Fe to establish St. Michael's College, which was built next door to the San Miguel Chapel. The chapel became part of that community. The college subsequently was renamed the College of Santa Fe, its charter expanded, and the campus moved to present-

day St. Michael's Drive. The former college buildings on Old Santa
Fe Trail now house state government offices, including the Tourism
Department, Visitor Center, and *New Mexico Magazine*. One of these
buildings is named for **Lew Wallace**.

NEW MEXICO CAPITOL

CONTINUE ON OLD SANTA FE TRAIL to the **New Mexico Capitol
(3)**, near the intersection of Paseo de Peralta and Old Santa Fe Trail.
This building, known as "the Roundhouse," was dedicated in 1966.
The governor's offices are in this building, along with the house and
senate chambers. It is built in the shape of the Zia sun symbol that also
appears on the New Mexico State flag. The local joke is that "they
built it round so that our politicians would never get cornered."

The state capitol and the governor's office play a role in several
books, including ***Serpent Gate*** (1998) by **Michael McGarrity** and
The Milagro Beanfield War (1974) by **John Nichols.**

John Nichols lives in Taos; *The Milagro Beanfield War*, the best-
known volume of a trilogy, is set mostly in a northern New Mexico
village. However, the issues addressed in the novel (water rights and
the impact of certain types of economic development on old New
Mexican families) are just as pertinent today in Santa Fe and many
other places in the state.

Actor-director **Robert Redford** (a frequent visitor to Santa Fe)
made the 1988 film based on this book, shot in Santa Fe and Truchas,
New Mexico. It is a truly enchanting production with an Oscar-
winning musical score composed by Santa Fe resident **Dave Grusin**.

Serpent Gate, in which a valuable piece of art is stolen from the
governor's office, is one of the many successful crime novels (or
mysteries) by Santa Fe writer Michael McGarrity. A former detective on the Santa Fe police force, McGarrity now writes full-time.

His tenth novel, ***Nothing But Trouble****,* was published in 2005. Critics and readers alike have praised McGarrity's work, comparing him with Tony Hillerman for his books set in New Mexico with a recurring detective character in each story. McGarrity's character is Kevin Kerney, a retired Santa Fe detective who is lured back into the business in the first book, *Tularosa* (1996), and who, in the most recent book, *Nothing But Trouble*, has become the city's top cop.

READ MORE ABOUT . . .

CONTEMPORARY MYSTERY WRITERS

Selected titles with Santa Fe settings:

* *Acquired Motives: A Dr. Sylvia Strange Novel*, by **Sarah Lovett**; also *A Desperate Silence* by the same author. Lovett has written a series of crime fiction novels about Dr. Sylvia Strange, who is a forensic psychologist, but only the first titles are set in Santa Fe and New Mexico.

* *The Fly on the Wall* is an early **Tony Hillerman** mystery featuring a journalist in Santa Fe who becomes caught up in political intrigues that lead him to Washington, D.C.

* *The Stolen Gods* by **Jake Page** is one of a series of novels featuring a blind sculptor who lives in Santa Fe.

* *Serpent Gate* and *Hermit's Peak* are two of **Michael McGarrity**'s crime novels with important scenes and plot actions set in Santa Fe. His detective, Kevin Kerney, has experience on the Santa Fe police force, as does author McGarrity.

* *Los Alamos* by **Joseph Kanon** involves murder, espionage, and unusual plot twists inside the Manhattan Project. The novel begins with a body discovered in Santa Fe.

* **Martha Grimes**, a popular American writer of British mysteries, has been a part-time resident of Santa Fe. In her novel

Rainbow's End, a series of deaths in England are related to events in Santa Fe, bringing Scotland Yard's Richard Jury to New Mexico.

- **Walter Satterthwait**'s novels feature a private eye named Joshua Croft. Some of these, including *A Wall of Glass* and *A Flower in the Desert,* have Santa Fe settings. He has also written historical mysteries involving Sir Arthur Conan Doyle (*Escapade*), Oscar Wilde (*Wilde West*), and Ernest Hemingway's Paris years (*Masquerade*).

- Santa Fe author **David Morrell** created the Rambo character in his 1972 novel, *First Blood.* Much of his fiction is in the thriller-horror-suspense category. A recent work, *Nightscape,* features a short story set in Santa Fe.

Other New Mexico mystery writers of note:

- Celebrated Chicano author **Rudolfo Anaya** began to write mysteries when he retired from teaching at the University of New Mexico. His Sonny Baca novels include *Zia Summer, Rio Grande Fall,* and *Shaman Winter.*

- **Judith Van Gieson** lives in Albuquerque, where both of her main characters live as well. Neil Hamel is the female attorney who stars in the mystery series, including *North of the Border* and *The Other Side of Death.* A newer series features an archivist-researcher at the University of New Mexico in *The Stolen Blue* and *Vanishing Point,* among others.

WITTER BYNNER'S HOME

PROCEED SOUTH ON OLD SANTA FE TRAIL about three blocks to Buena Vista Street, turn right, and enter the parking lot on the left (behind an adobe wall), at 342 East Buena Vista Street. This is the **Witter Bynner Home (4),** now operating as a bed-and-breakfast, the Inn of the Turquoise Bear. Owners Robert Frost and Ralph Bolton

*The home and gardens of the poet Witter Bynner, shown here
ca. 1938, have been restored by its present owners, who operate
it as a bed-and-breakfast, with an artistic bravado that commem-
orates the life and times of one of Santa Fe's literary lions.*

enjoy telling anecdotes about Bynner and his famous guests—if they
have time (depends on the time of day and how busy they are with
inn matters). They earned a 1999 Historic Preservation Award for their
restoration efforts to the historic estate. Selected copies of Bynner's
works and biography are on sale here.

Witter Bynner (1881–1968), who was "Hal" to his friends, was a
poet, essayist, and translator of Chinese literature as well as a strong

advocate of human rights. A Harvard graduate, he was independently wealthy and lived life on his own terms. The fact that he lived openly as a homosexual in the '20s and '30s may explain why many people outside Santa Fe have not heard of him. He could get away with such a "lifestyle" in Santa Fe, always tolerant of eccentrics and outsiders, more easily than in most places in the country at the time.

Not only did he thumb his nose at the social mores of the Eastern Establishment, he also angered the Literary Establishment when he and a friend published poems under pseudonyms that parodied the poetic fads of the day. This continued for two years before they were found out. What Bynner thought was great fun did not amuse those who were the brunt of the joke.

Bynner arrived in Santa Fe in 1922 to visit his friend, poet **Alice Corbin Henderson**, who was a resident and was being treated for tuberculosis at the Sunmount Sanitarium. He fell under the "spell" of Santa Fe and quickly decided to make it his home, renting the property on Buena Vista Street that he subsequently owned.

It was here that **D. H. Lawrence and his wife Frieda** spent their first night in an American home when they arrived in Santa Fe in 1922. They were traveling to Taos to be guests of **Mabel Dodge Luhan** but arrived exhausted from their rail journey from San Francisco. Even though Bynner was not acquainted with the Lawrences (Mabel had asked him to lodge them for the night), both parties had an immediate rapport. The following year, Bynner and his companion-secretary **Willard "Spud" Johnson** traveled with D. H. and Frieda to Mexico. Bynner later wrote about this trip in *Journey with Genius*, published in 1951.

Paul Horgan worked as Bynner's secretary for a time and later gave this description of him: "A man of commanding stature, splendid good looks, and infectious energy, he presided throughout five

Witter Bynner, shown here in 1932, was "Hal" to his friends, who were legion. Known for his wicked sense of humor, he was a serious poet, essayist, translator of Chinese literature, as well as a strong advocate of human rights.

decades, by common consent, over the cultural and convivial life in Santa Fe. His wit was a delight. It ranged through every degree of style, not disdaining ribaldry and brilliant puns, and it often took your breath away with its instant response to an unexpected lead." (Courtesy of the American Academy of Arts and Letters.)

Bynner's home was indeed the place where everyone visited sooner or later; his legendary wild parties went on until the wee hours of the morning. He acquired additions to his original small adobe home by buying adjoining properties when they became available. It eased complaints by the neighbors and he soon had a compound of multiple homes, typical of many of Santa Fe's oldest family estates.

The celebrity guest list at Bynner's home included **Willa Cather**, **Ansel Adams**, **Igor Stravinsky**, **Edna St. Vincent Millay** (to whom he was engaged for about twenty-four hours), **Robert Frost**, **W. H. Auden**, **Stephen Spender**, **Aldous Huxley**, **Clara Bow**, **Errol Flynn**, **Rita Hayworth**, **Christopher Isherwood**, **Martha Graham**, **Robert Oppenheimer**, **Georgia O'Keeffe**, **Mary Austin**, **Thornton Wilder**, and **J. B. Priestly,** among others. **Carl Sandburg**, **Mark Twain**, **O. Henry**, **Ezra Pound**, **A. E. Housman**, **Isadora Duncan**, and, briefly, **Henry James** were also among his friends and acquaintances.

His companion of some thirty years was **Robert Hunt**, who died in 1964. When Bynner died in 1968, he left his homes to St. John's College (in Santa Fe). The Buena Vista Street property later changed hands and was at one time the site of the **Witter Bynner Foundation for Poetry**, established by his estate. The foundation still funds creative endeavors.

As you leave the Inn of the Turquoise Bear, linger a moment at the corner of Buena Vista Street and Old Santa Fe Trail. You will observe the two- to three-block radius of the Witter Bynner home where several of his fellow writers and artists lived. These included **Gustave Baumann** (1881–1971), celebrated artist known for his masterful woodcut images, and **Oliver La Farge** (1901–1963), anthropologist and author.

La Farge's ***Laughing Boy: A Navajo Love Story*** (1929) won the Pulitzer Prize for Fiction; it was written before he moved to Santa Fe. The book arose out of his first trip to Navajo territory on a Harvard archaeological dig. He spent time in Santa Fe off and on for years and in 1941 made it his home, writing more books and a weekly column for the local newspaper, as well as becoming an advocate for historic preservation and Indian rights. La Farge's book **Santa Fe: The Autobiography of a Southwestern Town** (1959) is a selection of his columns and other news accounts from the *Santa Fe New Mexican*, the West's oldest newspaper, founded in 1849.

ARROYO TENORIO TO ACEQUIA MADRE

TURNING LEFT ON OLD SANTA FE TRAIL, go about one block and cross the street to the dirt road named **Arroyo Tenorio (5)**, which will take you to the **Acequia Madre**, another historic neighborhood of the Bohemian days. (Motor traffic cannot enter the one-way lane at this juncture, but walkers may proceed, with caution.)

A walk down the Arroyo Tenorio (about three blocks of narrow winding road) is like stepping back in time to the early part of the twentieth century, when the artists and writers were discovering Santa Fe. The charm of Santa Fe for many is this "frozen in time" experience that conjures up the Old World and the simpler life of days gone by. What can be jarring is meeting a Hummer or SUV on a narrow road such as this—and that is an everyday occurrence now.

Dirt roads are considered a status symbol of sorts in Santa Fe, a kind of "reverse snobbism." Many of the most expensive homes in the affluent neighborhoods are on unpaved roads, although the driveways leading to the homes may be paved.

The homes you see along this lane are built in the signature Santa Fe Style, probably of adobe, depending on the age of the house—and this neighborhood is one of the historic districts where design codes are enforced. In the old days, houses were built flush with the street, with interior courtyards, or *placitas*, behind adobe walls. (The Santa Fe Garden Club's annual "Behind Adobe Walls" tour is always popular because it affords an opportunity to see lovely gardens and details of homes that are not visible to passersby.)

When you emerge at the intersection of Garcia Street and Acequia Madre, you will see the beginning of another historic neighborhood where people like **B. B. Dunne** lived and where **Paul Horgan** stayed in rental accommodations during the summers. This area has many vacation rentals alongside the homes of permanent and part-time residents, which are occupied mostly during the summer.

Garcia Street Books and *Downtown Subscription*

You might wish to rest a moment, take refreshment, and browse for books at **Garcia Street Books (B1)** and at **Downtown Subscription (B1)**. Both are places frequented by local residents and writers. Downtown Subscription offers an extensive collection of newspapers and magazines from around the world, along with a coffee bar. Garcia Street Books, next door, is a popular independent bookstore that features local authors as well as many of the nation's most respected writers who include Santa Fe on book tours.

ACEQUIA MADRE TO CAMINO DEL MONTE SOL

FOLLOW **Acequia Madre to Camino del Monte Sol (6)** as it winds around, with the old *acequia* [ah-say'kee-ya] running alongside. An acequia is an irrigation ditch; *acequia madre* means "the mother ditch," and this one dates from Santa Fe's earliest days.

The picturesque adobe homes of yesteryear are still found in Santa Fe's old neighborhoods adjoining Canyon Road. The area is popular for vacation rentals and second homes, scattered amongst the longtime residents, including many of today's writers and artists.

The Spanish used ditch irrigation for centuries, a practice probably influenced by the Moors who inhabited Spain for almost eight hundred years (*acequia* is a Moorish word, integrated into Spanish). The Indians in the Southwest also used ditch irrigation, but the Spanish colonists introduced them to new techniques to manage water use, along with irrigation laws. For example, each acequia, or ditch district, elects a *mayordomo* to supervise and schedule use of the water, which is regulated by opening (and closing) metal gates that control flow to various tributaries.

The acequia system is still honored and maintained in many rural areas and towns in northern New Mexico; it is used to water crops and gardens. The acequia madre in this Santa Fe neighborhood still flows and still operates by the old Spanish laws. Residents pay an annual fee for use of the water for their gardens and they are required to help with cleaning out the acequia every spring.

A good book on acequias and the rural traditions of *el norte* is **Mayordomo: Chronicle of an Acequia in Northern New Mexico** (1988) by **Stanley G. Crawford**, a respected New Mexico author (and farmer) living in Dixon, New Mexico, north of Santa Fe. He helped establish the Santa Fe Farmers Market.

(Motor traffic must turn right on Abeyta Street, then left on Camino Poniente, before the Acequia Madre intersects with Camino del Monte Sol. Walkers may use that route or continue straight on Acequia Madre; either way, you will arrive at the intersection with Camino del Monte Sol.)

MARY AUSTIN'S HOME

TURN RIGHT ON THE CAMINO DEL MONTE SOL and walk up about two blocks; 439 Camino del Monte Sol is on the left. This is **Mary Austin's Home (7)**, her Casa Querida (Beloved House), now occupied by Chiaroscuro Contemporary Art.

Mary Hunter Austin (1868–1934), playwright, poet, and novelist, moved to Santa Fe in 1924, although she had been visiting here since 1918. In these years, she had become involved in the town's artistic life—as well as various causes: notably, Indian rights and historic preservation. Already a respected author who had published many books, Austin had lived in Carmel-by-the-Sea, California, as well as New York, and had traveled widely in Europe.

Two of her books about New Mexico are **The Land of Journeys' Ending** (1924) and **Starry Adventure** (1931), a novel.

Both Mary Austin and Ernest Thompson Seton, shown at her Santa Fe home in 1927, have been called naturalist writers.

Austin helped found three organizations that are still prominent in Santa Fe: the New Mexico Association on Indian Affairs (now SWAIA, Southwestern Association for Indian Art), the Spanish Colonial Arts Society, and the Old Santa Fe Association. Along with Frank Applegate and others, Austin fought to preserve the Santuario de Chimayó and other historic churches in the region.

In the early 1920s, Austin was at the forefront of the Santa Fe and Taos writers' and artists' colonies that helped defeat the infamous Bursum Bill. In 1922, Senator Holm Bursum (New Mexico) introduced federal legislation that would have denied Indians the rights to their lands, handing the lands over to Hispanos and Anglos who claimed rights. The ensuing uproar surprised New Mexico's elected officials at the time, who underestimated the influence and the emotions of the writers and artists who got involved, convincing the Pueblos to close ranks and form a united front in what some have called the Second Pueblo Revolt.

Oliver La Farge points out that the *Santa Fe New Mexican*'s edition on September 20, 1922, alerted readers that the Bursum Bill was being published in its entirety so that everyone would know what it proposed. Readers were urged to read it carefully and understand its "tremendous, far-reaching importance."

The editorial writer added, "Not since the days of Custer has it been necessary to 'protect' non-Indians in this country against the Indian. The steady pressure of encroachment has borne them backward and further backward everywhere. The Indian is the most historic of all under dogs." (*Santa Fe: The Autobiography of a Southwestern Town*, by Oliver La Farge, 1959.)

This walk illustrates the closeness—and the proximity in residences—of the early Santa Fe writers and artists. They lived in adjoining neighborhoods; they partied together, joined forces to improve their community, and often collaborated in their work.

Austin wrote a children's book of poetry, *The Children Sing in the Far West*, printed in 1928, with illustrations by her neighbor **Gerald Cassidy**, an early Santa Fe artist. (His Canyon Road home is also noted on the Walk.)

Austin wrote the introduction to **Native Tales of New Mexico,** authored by her neighbor **Frank Applegate**, and prepared it for publication in 1932 after his death the previous year. With the photographer **Ansel Adams**, a frequent visitor to Santa Fe, she collaborated on a 1930 book about Taos Pueblo.

Many literary tributes were published about Mary Austin when she died in 1934. Among them was a profile in the *Saturday Review of*

Literature by Santa Fe author **Elizabeth Shepley Sergeant. T. M. Pearce** has written two biographies of this lady of letters: *The Beloved House*, published in 1940, and *Mary Hunter Austin*, published in 1965.

Truly, Santa Fe was a small town then, but it was peopled with brilliant minds and great talents, and characterized by a sophistication that set it apart from other towns in New Mexico—or of comparable size anywhere. The same could be said of Santa Fe today.

CB

Other Neighbors on the Camino

Across the street and up on the right is El Caminito, a lane off of Camino del Monte Sol, where **Frank Applegate** (1882–1931) lived. He was an artist as well as a writer who had purchased the historic De La Peña House and, with some training in architecture, had enlarged it. Applegate helped define the Spanish Pueblo Revival style and used his skills to help other artists build or restore homes, including **Los Cinco Pintores** whose homes are farther up on Camino del Monte Sol (#8 on this walk). Poet **Alice Corbin Henderson** (1881–1949) and her artist husband **William Penhallow Henderson** (1877–1943), called "Whippy," also lived on Monte Sol; their home is now a private residence near Camino Santander, farther up the street.

The Camino del Monte Sol (Sun Mountain Road) is named for the **Sunmount Sanitarium** that was located farther out at the intersection of Camino del Monte Sol with the Old Santa Fe Trail. Originally built as a tent city in 1903, Sunmount was part health spa and part resort, but after Dr. Frank Mera took it over in the late '20s, it became known nationwide as a premier facility for the treatment of tuberculosis. When Mera died in 1970, the facility was sold to the archdiocese of Santa Fe. Today it is the Carmelite Monastery and Immaculate Heart of Mary Retreat and Conference Center.

Alice Corbin Henderson was receiving treatment at Sunmount when poet Witter Bynner visited her in 1922. Struggling with a bout of influenza, he checked himself into the sanitarium. The rest and treatment not only restored his health but also gave him time to discover that he wanted to make his home in Santa Fe. This experience was not uncommon; architect **John Gaw Meem** and artist **Carlos Vierra** followed the same path here, among others. Vierra also got involved in historic preservation and helped restore the Palace of the Governors.

William Penhallow Henderson and Alice Corbin Henderson pose in costume, 1932.

The Hendersons came to Santa Fe in 1916 from Chicago, making them among the earliest of the creative people who would become the Santa Fe art colony. She was a distinguished poet and one of the founders of *Poetry* magazine. He was an established artist in various media who became a builder and architect. They were regarded as the guiding forces of the Santa Fe group for many years.

Six landscape murals by William Penhallow Henderson are still displayed on the interior of the U.S. court house (next door to the main post office) in downtown Santa Fe. These were painted during the '30s as part of the New Deal's WPA (Works Progress Administration) Art Project that put many of the writers and artists in Santa Fe to work during the Depression.

Taking tea at La Fonda was the custom of 1930s Santa Fe society. La Fonda was the place to see and to be seen—and to learn the latest gossip.

Henderson also became interested in the preservation of adobe buildings, designed and remodeled a number of them, and, like his friend Frank Applegate, helped promote Spanish Pueblo Revival architecture.

Readers may get acquainted with the work of Alice Corbin Henderson through the reissue of ***Red Earth: Poems of New Mexico*** (2003), originally published in 1920. The book pairs the poems with paintings and photographs from the permanent collections of the Museum of Fine Arts.

ᙏ

Links Between the Writers and Artists of Santa Fe and Taos

The Hendersons' daughter Alice married Mabel Dodge Luhan's son John Evans, creating another link between the Santa Fe and Taos artists' and writers' colonies. While **Mabel Dodge Luhan** (1879–1962) was the acknowledged leader of the Taos colonies since her arrival in 1916, the Santa Fe groups were influenced by several: namely, Witter Bynner, Mary Austin, and the Hendersons.

Mabel had a very strong and possessive personality, often competing for the attention of the writers and artists who first came to New Mexico at her invitation. She became jealous of Bynner because the Lawrences were so fond of him and invited him to travel with them to Mexico. It could be said that a rivalry sprang up between the Santa Fe and Taos groups, with each vying for the reputation as "the best place for writers and artists." Each place had its distinctive characteristics and people—and the gossip flew back and forth as quickly as possible in the '30s and '40s.

Paul Horgan described it this way in his last book, ***Tracings: A Book of Partial Portraits*** (1993):

Between Santa Fe and Taos there was a sense of rival constituencies, and sensitive persons tended to be loyal to the powers, virtues, and dangers of one place or the other. Santa Fe was more worldly, more sophisticated. Taos believed itself to be animated by an energy of place that was actually occult. So it came to be that the atmospheric culture of Santa Fe and Taos could be likened to a cloud bank full of lightning strikes of gossip in constant discharge.

Mabel Dodge Luhan was an author and she dabbled in painting. However, she felt that her greatest talent was in bringing together creative people and setting the scene for their creativity to blossom. In addition to her memoirs, Mabel wrote **Lorenzo in Taos** (1932) about D. H. Lawrence, and **Winter in Taos** (1935), among other titles.

Independently wealthy, she had married several times and always attracted writers and artists to her home wherever she lived. At her salons in Europe and New York City, Mabel had become friendly with many literary and artistic figures such as **Gertrude Stein**, **John (Jack) Reed**, **Eugene O'Neill**, **Alfred Stieglitz**, **John Sloan**, and **Georgia O'Keeffe**, among others.

Lois Palken Rudnick's biography, **Mabel Dodge Luhan: New Woman, New Worlds** (1984) is a good place to start to learn more about this fascinating woman and her era. Also recommended is **Mabel's Santa Fe and Taos: Bohemian Legends, 1900–1950**, by **Elmo Baca** (2000).

WILL SHUSTER'S HOME

BACK ON CAMINO DEL MONTE SOL, continue to walk uphill to number 550, the adobe house with turquoise trim. This is **Will Shuster's Home (8)**. He was one of **Los Cinco Pintores** (the Five Painters), best remembered today for creating the giant puppet **Zozobra** (Old Man Gloom), which is burned in effigy each year at the Santa Fe Fiesta.

Artist Will Shuster shows off his creation, Zozobra, or Old Man Gloom.

Shuster (1893–1969) was something of a prankster as well as a talented artist. He and several artist friends dreamed up the idea of burning Zozobra as a symbolic act that would burn up all the worries and woes of the good citizens of Santa Fe in an annual ritual. Shuster is credited with the design of Zozobra, who first appeared at the Santa Fe Fiesta in 1926.

The ritual continues today, with many Santa Feans donating papers (the documents of a messy divorce, for example) and related material to put inside Zozobra. All is torched at a climactic moment, attended by fire dancers and roars from the crowd, followed by raucous cheers when Old Man Gloom goes up in flames. It echoes barbaric rites of the past; in fact, the Aztecs performed cleansing fire rituals that were prescribed every fifty-two years, according to their calendar and beliefs.

Los Cinco Pintores is the name given to five young artists who all arrived in Santa Fe about the same time. They organized themselves as a group in 1921 and soon made their debut with an exhibition at the Museum of Fine Arts. They had become so friendly that they built their adobe homes near each other on what was then called Telephone Road, now the Camino del Monte Sol. They referred to themselves as "the five little nuts who live in mud huts." Their homes were side by side, all in a row; all are private residences now.

In addition to Shuster, the artists were **Willard Nash** (1898–1943), **Fremont Ellis** (1897–1985), **Josef Bakos** (1891–1977), and **Wladyslaw (Walter) Mruk** (1885–1942). Although prominent in Santa Fe, these artists never gained the national stature of the **Taos Society of Artists**, but most of the works of Los Cinco Pintores have gained in value over the years.

Winfield Townley Scott (1910–1968), a distinguished poet and editor who spent his later years in Santa Fe, describes living on the Camino in the mid-1950s:

> *Our house on the Camino del Monte Sol is one of several built in the 1920s by the five young artists who called themselves the cinco pintores. . . . The Camino—there are caminos this and that in town but ours is known as The Camino—is one of the routes of the sight-seeing buses. . . . Part of its charm is alleged to be the road itself, unpaved, dusty, corduroy, and, in wet weather, greasy. Its real charm lies in its gated walls, its rambling houses, its great view of the Sangre de Cristos. . . . There are two or three imposing houses along the Camino, but mostly we run from humble to middle size. I know of one painter, one photographer, one sculptor, and a couple of writers now living on this road; the other residents include . . . a dealer in antiques and real estate, a perfume manufacturer, and a handful of Spanish-Americans, among them Jesus Rios, from whose wood yard at the foot of the Camino we all buy our fireplace piñon. There are now many new "developments" in and around the town, but the Camino is like almost any older Santa Fe street, in that different races and different economic strata are all mixed together. There is a railroad track in Santa Fe, but no right and wrong side of it.*

From Scott's 1957 work, *Exiles and Fabrications*,
excerpted in *The Spell of New Mexico*,
edited by Tony Hillerman, 1976.

To reach Canyon Road, go back down Camino Monte Sol to the intersection with Acequia Madre. Because this walk requires traveling some distances, **two options** are offered: 1) skip the next two sites and go directly to **Canyon Road (11)**, which is about one mile long and has two stops related to this walk, along with many galleries and shops worth investigating, or 2) turn right on Acequia Madre to do the loop that will take you back to Canyon Road, which will add about three-quarters of a mile.

ACEQUIA MADRE AND DON MIGUEL

THE 1970 MOVIE ***Red Sky at Morning,*** which was based on **Richard Bradford**'s novel of the same name, was partially filmed at the house on the right at the corner of **Acequia Madre and Don Miguel (9)**. The surrounding neighborhood served as background for much of the film's action in residential areas. Unfortunately, this delightful film, starring Richard Thomas and Claire Bloom, is not available for home viewing.

Red Sky at Morning (1968) is a touching and often humorous coming-of-age story set in Santa Fe during World War II. The *Washington Post* called it "a sort of *Catcher in the Rye* out West." Somewhat autobiographical, the book presents a young hero from Mobile, Alabama (Bradford lived in New Orleans), who has spent summers in Sagrado (the fictional name for Santa Fe) for many years. His family's move to New Mexico just before his last year of high school presents him with several challenges—and the reader sees Santa Fe through the eyes of a newcomer as well as those whose families have been here for generations:

> *I had been away from Sagrado for seven summers, but nothing had changed. Nobody had built a defense plant there, or an Army base. There was talk of something warlike going on at Los Alamos, up in the Jemez Mountains, where there had once been a rustic boys' school, but we assumed it was just another boon-doggle. "They're manufacturing the*

front part of horses up there," Dad suggested, "and shipping them to Washington for final assembly."

The streets in Sagrado were a little pockier than I remembered, and the few cars were fewer. While Mobile was growing and spreading out, raw, new and ugly, Sagrado protected itself, as it had for more than three hundred years, by being nonessential. That's the best way to get through a war: Don't be big and strong, be hard to find.

Bradford himself, a resident of Santa Fe from 1961 until his death in 2002, lived just up the street at one time, at 948 Acequia Madre, near where the street flows into Canyon Road. This is "turn-left-at-the-sleeping-dog" territory, where street signs were scarce or nonexistent in times past. Even today many little dirt lanes are unmarked; one nearby is called the Camino sin Nombre (road with no name).

Richard Bradford once used the colorful directive to guide a visitor to his home in the late 1950s. **Pen La Farge** chose it for the title of his 2001 book, ***Turn Left at the Sleeping Dog***, which includes a lengthy interview with Bradford recalling the episode. Bradford continued to write for local publications and published another novel, ***So Far From Heaven***, in 1973.

As you continue along Acequia Madre, just after the sharp curve, you will see a narrow dirt lane off to the right; several mailboxes have numbers. Just up the lane is the house at 986 (now a private residence) where writer **Donald Hamilton** lived for many years. He is the author of spy fiction and Western novels who created **Matt Helm**, the secret agent portrayed by Dean Martin in film. Hamilton, a prolific writer, was reported to be living in Sweden (at age ninety) in 2006. His Matt Helm series began with ***Death of a Citizen*** (1960), containing scenes in Santa Fe, and continued until 1993.

Hamilton's short story *Ambush at Blanco Canyon* was adapted for the big screen and became the 1958 film *The Big Country,* later published as a novel under that same name. The motion picture starred Gregory Peck and Charlton Heston, and it was a box office success. Although it was not filmed in New Mexico, the novel's setting is in the borderlands of Texas–New Mexico–Mexico, and its treatment of land grants and water rights is relevant today.

FROM NOVEL TO BIG SCREEN: FILMS BASED ON NEW MEXICO LITERATURE

New Mexico's film industry dates from 1898 and is thriving today. Many classic films, not based on New Mexico literature, have been made here, including *The Grapes of Wrath* (1940), *Butch Cassidy and the Sundance Kid* (1968), *Easy Rider* (1969), and *Silkwood* (1983).

All of the following titles are based on New Mexico literature and were filmed in New Mexico. They are listed chronologically by film release date.

1947   *The Sea of Grass*, based on Conrad Richter's novel of the same name.

1947   *Ride the Pink Horse*, based on Dorothy Hughes' novel of the same name.

1948   *Four Faces West*, based on Eugene Manlove Rhodes' novel *Pasó por Aquí* (*They Passed This Way*).

1955   *Oklahoma!* the film version of the Broadway musical, based on the 1931 play, *Green Grow the Lilacs*, by Lynn Riggs, who lived in Santa Fe in the 1920s.

1958   *The Nine Lives of Elfego Baca*, based on various books about this New Mexico legend.

(Cont'd on next page)

(From Novel to Big Screen, cont'd)

1962 *Lonely Are the Brave*, based on Edward Abbey's novel
      The Brave Cowboy.

1964 *A Distant Trumpet*, based on Paul Horgan's novel of the
      same name.

1966 *And Now, Miguel*, based on Joseph Krumgold's novel of
      the same name.

1970 *Red Sky at Morning*, based on Richard Bradford's novel
      of the same name.

1972 *House Made of Dawn*, based on N. Scott Momaday's
      novel of the same name.

1988 *The Milagro Beanfield War*, based on John Nichols'
      novel of the same name.

1998 *The Hi-Lo Country*, based on Max Evans' novel of the
      same name.

2000 *All the Pretty Horses*, based on Cormac McCarthy's
      novel of the same name.

Note: Three of Tony Hillerman's novels were translated to the
small screen in 2002–2004 when the **PBS Mystery Series**
broadcast *Skinwalkers*, *Coyote Waits*, and *A Thief of Time*. These
were filmed in Arizona and Utah, near the New Mexico border,
a region called "Navajoland."

GERALD CASSIDY PLACITA

STRAIGHT AHEAD, where the street meets Canyon Road, turn left.
After a block or so, you will see 924 Canyon Road on the left, the
Gerald Cassidy Placita (10). This residential compound, now
privately owned, was the home of the painter and his wife, **Ina
Sizer Cassidy**, a poet, writer, and lecturer.

Gerald Cassidy (1879–1934) was one of the first artists to live permanently on Canyon Road; his first residence in 1915 was at 550 Canyon Road. His work is quite valuable today. One of Cassidy's paintings was the centerpiece of a recent exhibition at the Museum of Fine Arts. His portrait of a Pueblo man in a white wrap near an adobe wall, *Cui Bono? (Who Benefits?)*, was painted about 1911 and has been in the museum collection for many years.

CANYON ROAD

CONTINUE DOWN **Canyon Road (11)** to the intersection with Camino del Monte Sol. From this point on, you will experience a one-mile walk encompassing about one hundred of Santa Fe's two hundred (plus) galleries. In this old part of Santa Fe, once home to generations of Spanish families who farmed the area, gentrification in the 1960s came at a high price. Families were forced to sell because of high property taxes, and many artists who had been living there, selling their work out of their homes, moved away.

Before the Spanish came, this old road was an Indian trail that went over the Sangre de Cristo (blood of Christ) mountains, linking the rural area to the Pecos Pueblo. Later, the Spanish named it El Camino del Cañon (the road of the canyon). From the early 1800s well into the twentieth century, Canyon Road was the conduit from the mountains for transporting split firewood on the backs of burros to present-day **Burro Alley**, where it would be sold.

While a few residences still remain among the galleries and shops, the **Upper Canyon Road,** extending about four miles east of the Canyon Road and Alameda Street intersection, is mostly residential. At the end of Upper Canyon Road is the historic home of the painter **Randall Davey** (1887–1964), who was part of the Santa Fe art colony. It is now headquarters to the Randall Davey Audubon Center.

Since the late '60s, Canyon Road has been the mecca of Santa Fe art, with fine restaurants and old-world ambience combined with boutique shops and art galleries of all kinds. On this street alone, one could find twelfth-century pueblo pottery, nineteenth-century Plains Indians moccasins, abstract expressionist paintings, handmade jewelry of precious metals, Tibetan Buddhist arts, kinetic sculpture, Ming Dynasty urns, traditional cowboy art and sculpture—and much more.

Canyon Road also boasts two of Santa Fe's finest—and most expensive—restaurants. **Gerónimo**, at 724 Canyon Road, is housed in the historic Rafael Borrego House and takes its name from an early resident, Gerónimo (Jerome) López, and not the Apache chief.

The Compound Restaurant, at 653 Canyon Road, is set back from the street, operating in a former residence that was converted to a restaurant. The interior design was done by the late **Alexander Girard** (1907–1993), whose impressive collection of folk art occupies its own wing on Museum Hill at the **International Folk Art Museum**, one of the "must see" places in Santa Fe.

EL ZAGUÁN

About midway on the right is 545 Canyon Road, **El Zaguán (12)**, a fine old home that now contains the offices of the **Historic Santa Fe Foundation**, with some private apartments for long-time residents.

"One of the architectural treasures of New Mexico, this rambling old hacienda and its garden stretch more than 300 feet along lower Canyon Road." (*Old Santa Fe Today*, 4th edition, 1991, published by the Historic Santa Fe Foundation.) Its name comes from the Spanish word for the long, covered corridor that runs from the garden to an open patio. **James L. Johnson**, a successful merchant of Santa Fe Trail days, acquired it in 1849 and expanded the house as his residence, adding a private chapel and "a semidetached room overlooking the west garden for his library, said to have been the largest in the territory."

The garden is named for novelist and anthropologist **Adolph Bandelier**, who designed it. The peony bushes, imported from China more than one hundred years ago, still bloom, providing one of Santa Fe's loveliest annual garden sightings. Johnson planted the two horse chestnut trees that stand like sentinels and are now regarded as local landmarks.

The lovely garden at El Zaguán is named for Adolph Bandelier, who designed it.

ADOLPH BANDELIER'S HOME

FOLLOW CANYON ROAD to its end at the Paseo de Peralta, turning left for one-quarter block, to the last stop on this walk: **Adolph Bandelier's Home (13)**, now the location of a prominent gallery of American Indian Art—Sherwood's Spirit of America. The building is Territorial in style and has been extensively enlarged and remodeled.

Bandelier (1840–1914) has been mentioned repeatedly on the literary trails of Santa Fe. He lived in this house from 1882 to 1892 while he did research in New Mexico, Arizona, and Mexico. In the early 1880s, he explored the ruins and cliff dwellings of ancient peoples of the Pajarito Plateau near present-day Los Alamos. That place is now called Bandelier National Monument, so designated by President Woodrow Wilson in 1914, shortly before Bandelier's death in Seville, Spain.

According to *Old Santa Fe Today* (1991), "He was the first scholar to attempt a comprehensive, scientific study of the archaeology, ethnography, and historical documentation of the New Mexico Indians. He traveled thousands of miles on foot and horseback and often lived for weeks at a time in Indian villages." Bandelier's 1890 novel ***The Delight Makers*** was his effort to imagine the life of the prehistoric Pueblo people who had lived in such a place.

During his time in Santa Fe, Bandelier became a good friend of **Archbishop Lamy**, visiting him often at his retreat north of town, the present-day Bishop's Lodge Ranch Resort & Spa, after Lamy's retirement. Perhaps it was the bond of their European birth—Bandelier was born in Switzerland—that first drew them together, but the friendship lasted until Lamy's death in 1888.

This is the last stop on the Old Santa Fe Trail to Canyon Road Walk. You can make your way back to the Plaza or La Fonda Hotel by following Alameda Street to Old Santa Fe Trail, and then go right for another two blocks.

RESOURCES

New Mexico Literary Timeline

CB

* National and international events

BC

ca 20,000   Sandia people may have been the earliest people in what is now New Mexico.

ca 10,000   Petroglyphs dating to this time have been discovered in the Big Smokey Valley of Nevada; it is likely that New Mexico's petroglyphs also date from this time.

9,600–8,800   Clovis points (from Clovis, New Mexico), tools of Paleo-Indian hunters (known as Clovis people) who pursued ice age mammoths, camels, bison, and horses, date to this time. These people were ancestral to the Folsom culture and were believed to have arrived across a land bridge from Asia.

900★   Evidence of an early writing system dating from this period has been found in Mexico. The Olmecs (1200–400 BC) leave symbols chipped in stone and pottery, believed to be the first writing system in the Americas. Those symbols are later adopted by other native cultures like the Maya.

ca 200★   Maya hieroglyphs; AD 250–900 is Classic Maya period.

AD

ca 800–1300   Classic Pueblo period of Anasazi culture; cliff dwellings, and highly developed Chaco civilization.

912–961★   Arab Spain becomes center of learning.

1066★   The Norman Invasion of William the Conqueror; last Saxon king, Harold II, is defeated at Battle of Hastings.

1195–1240   Ancient Pueblo culture lives in area of present-day Santa Fe.

1231★   The Inquisition begins: Pope Gregory IX assigns Dominicans to combat heresy. Ferdinand and Isabella establish Spanish Inquisition (1478), forcing conversion or expulsion of Spanish Jews (1492) and conversion of Moors (1499). Inquisition in Portugal (1531). First Protestants burned at the stake in Spain (1543).

ca 1325★	Aztecs establish Tenochtitlán on site of modern Mexico City; peak of Muslim culture in Spain.
1492★	Moors conquered in Spain by troops of Ferdinand and Isabella. Columbus becomes first European to encounter Caribbean islands.
1521★	Spanish conquest of Aztecs by Hernan Cortés.
1550–1700★	Transition from Maya hieroglyphs to the use of the Roman alphabet taught by the Spanish priests; the *Popol Vuh,* sacred Maya text, is written in secret.
1582	This area first called New Mexico (la Nueva México) by the Spanish explorers.
1598	Juan de Oñate founds San Juan de los Caballeros, northwest of Santa Fe, as the first capital of New Mexico.
1599	Battle at Acoma between Indians and Spaniards leaves lasting resentment, sowing seeds of the Pueblo Revolt of 1680.
1605★	Cervantes' *Don Quixote de la Mancha* is published.
ca 1605–7	Santa Fe is established as the capital of New Mexico.
1607★	Jamestown, Virginia, is established, the first permanent English colony on American mainland.
1609–10	Governor Pedro de Peralta begins construction on the Palace of the Governors.
1610	Captain Gaspar Pérez de Villagrá publishes *Historia de la Nueva México,* the first epic poem written about New Mexico.
1626	Spanish Inquisition is established in New Mexico.
1680	Pueblo Indian Revolt; Spanish survivors flee to El Paso del Norte.
1690–92★	Salem witch trials in Massachusetts.
1692–93	Don Diego de Vargas recolonizes Santa Fe; Spanish leadership returns to New Mexico.
1712	The Santa Fe Fiesta is celebrated for the first time, commemorating the reconquest of New Mexico by the Spanish in 1693; it is the oldest community celebration still in existence.

1756–66	Witch trials in Abiquiú, New Mexico.
1787★	The Constitution of the United States is signed.
1806–7	Zebulon Pike leads first Anglo-American expedition into New Mexico; later publishes account of way of life in New Mexico.
1821	Mexico declares independence from Spain; first wagons arrive in Santa Fe over the Santa Fe Trail.
1832	Antonio Barreiro, Santa Fe delegate to the Mexican congress, decries the lack of a press in the territory and advocates acquiring one to promote literacy.
1834	First printing press arrives in New Mexico.
1834★	Spanish Inquisition is abolished.
1835	The first book printed in New Mexico, the *Cuaderno de Ortigrafía* (a school spelling primer) is published by Padre Antonio José Martínez of Taos.
1836★	Mexican army besieges Texans in Alamo; entire garrison wiped out. Texans gain independence from Mexico after winning Battle of San Jacinto.
1844	*Commerce of the Prairies* by Josiah Gregg (2 volumes) is published.
1844★	Telegraph is invented.
1846	Mexican-American War begins; Stephen Watts Kearny annexes New Mexico to the United States.
1847	Taos Rebellion against the U.S. military; Governor Charles Bent is killed.
1848	Treaty of Guadalupe-Hidalgo ends Mexican-American War; Mexico cedes claims to Texas, California, Arizona, New Mexico, Utah, and Nevada.
1849	*The Santa Fe New Mexican*, the West's oldest newspaper, is established.
1849★	The California Gold Rush begins.

1850   New Mexico (which included present-day Arizona, southern Colorado, southern Utah and southern Nevada) is designated a territory. Santa Fe population put at 4,846 and population of territory at 61,547 by territorial census.

1851   Reverend Jean Baptiste Lamy arrives in New Mexico; establishes schools, hospitals, and orphanages throughout the territory, along with ecclesiastical reforms. He becomes a bishop in 1853 with the elevation of the New Mexico Vicariate to the Diocese of Santa Fe, and an archbishop in 1875.

1856   *El Gringo, or New Mexico and Her People*, written by W. W. H. Davis, is published; reprinted by Rydal, Santa Fe, 1938. Santa Fe Literary Club is formed, dedicated to the expansion of knowledge.

1862–68   The relocation of Navajos and Apaches, known as the "Long Walk," forces them to trek to Bosque Redondo; they are finally allowed to return to their homelands after thousands die of disease and starvation.

1867   Padre Antonio José Martínez dies; a memorial statue of him is dedicated in Taos in 2006.

1869★   First U.S. transcontinental rail route is completed at Promontory Point in northern Utah.

1878–81   Lincoln County War in southeast New Mexico pits cattle barons against homesteaders; this conflict, along with the Santa Fe Ring and Billy the Kid, are major challenges that Lew Wallace confronts as New Mexico's territorial governor during this time.

1878   The railroad arrives in New Mexico, bypassing Santa Fe by some twenty miles to the south, and opening full-scale trade and migration from the East and Midwest.

1880   Lew A. Wallace's *Ben Hur: A Tale of the Christ* is published.

1880   Adolph Bandelier begins a survey of Southwestern archeological ruins.

1881   Billy the Kid shot by Sheriff Pat Garrett in Fort Sumner.

1883 Charles F. Lummis publishes *The Land of Poco Tiempo*, declaring New Mexico "the anomaly of the Republic."

1886 Geronimo, Apache Indian chief, surrenders, ending the Apache wars in southern New Mexico and Arizona.

1888 Archbishop Lamy dies and is buried in a crypt at the St. Francis Cathedral. *The Santa Fe New Mexican* urges teaching of English in public schools be compulsory.

1890 Adolph Bandelier's novel, *The Delight Makers*, is published.

1891 The Fifteen Club, a small literary society, is organized in Santa Fe, the first women's club in Santa Fe, and the second in New Mexico Territory.

1894★ Edison's kinetoscope is given first public showing in New York City.

1898 *Indian Day School,* by Thomas A. Edison, is the first movie filmed in New Mexico; Spanish-American War begins and Teddy Roosevelt comes to New Mexico to recruit soldiers for his Rough Riders Regiment.

1898 Artists Ernest Blumenschein and Bert Phillips accidentally discover Taos and decide to stay. Their reports of the area spark a migration of artists to New Mexico.

1903 Sunmount Sanitarium established in Santa Fe, where many writers and artists received treatment for tuberculosis.

1909 The Palace of the Governors is renovated for the first time; becomes the History Museum of the Museum of New Mexico.

1912 New Mexico admitted to the Union as the forty-seventh state, ending sixty-four years as a U.S. territory.

1914 President Woodrow Wilson designates Bandelier National Monument, shortly before Adolph Bandelier dies in Seville, Spain.

1915 Taos Society of Artists formed with original six members.

1916 Pancho Villa raids Columbus, New Mexico. Painter William Penhallow Henderson and his wife, poet Alice

Corbin Henderson, settle in Santa Fe. Mabel Dodge Luhan arrives in Taos and decides to make it her home.

1917 School of American Research is founded in Santa Fe. New Museum of Fine Arts is dedicated. Georgia O'Keeffe visits New Mexico for the first time.

1918 Worldwide influenza epidemic strikes New Mexico.

1919 A $200,000 subscription campaign provides money for a new hotel that will become La Fonda in Santa Fe. Santa Fe Fiesta revived. Mary Austin launches the Community Theater of Santa Fe.

1919★ The "Vicious Circle" of writers known as the Algonquin Round Table begins daily lunches at Manhattan's Algonquin Hotel.

1920 Adoption of the 19th Amendment gives women the right to vote. U.S. Census reports New Mexico population as 360,350.

1921 Los Cinco Pintores established as a group; within months, they hold their first exhibition in Santa Fe at the Museum of Fine Arts.

1922 Witter Bynner first visits Santa Fe and decides to make it his home.

1926 Old Santa Fe Association formed by John Gaw Meem, Mary Austin, and others. Fred Harvey acquires Erna Fergusson's Koshare tours, establishing Indian Detours, operating out of La Fonda, a Harvey Hotel. Will Shuster's Zozobra, Old Man Gloom, is first burned in effigy at the Santa Fe Fiesta.

1927 Willa Cather's *Death Comes for the Archbishop* is published. Roberta Robey's Villagra Book Shop opens in Sena Plaza.

1929 Oliver La Farge's *Laughing Boy* is published; wins Pulitzer Prize for Fiction.

1930–43 Great Depression, Federal New Deal, and WPA funds provide employment for many, including New Mexico artists and writers, and pay for construction of numerous public buildings.

1935 *My Life on the Frontier, 1864–1882,* the first of three memoirs by Miguel A. Otero (1859–1944), is published. Otero is the first Hispano to serve as New Mexico territorial governor, 1897–1906.

1942   Frank Waters writes *The Man Who Killed the Deer.*

1942–45   New Mexico soldiers serving in the 200th Coast Artillery during World War II are captured by the Japanese and forced to endure the Bataan Death March, with some 900 men (about half of the group) dying. Navajo "code talkers" are influential in helping end the war. Secret atomic laboratory established at Los Alamos.

1945   World's first atomic bomb detonated at Trinity Site in southern New Mexico after its development at Los Alamos; two bombs dropped on Japan, one on Hiroshima and the other on Nagasaki, effectively ending the Second World War.

1945   Santa Fe has two art galleries.

1946   *Ride the Pink Horse*, by Dorothy B. Hughes, is published; adapted as a motion picture in 1947.

1947   UFO allegedly crashes between Roswell and Corona; believers claim U.S. government institutes massive cover-up of the incident.

1948   American Indians win the right to vote in national and state elections (only in New Mexico and two other states). Ruth Laughlin Barker writes *The Wind Leaves No Shadow*, based on the life of Doña Tules Barcelo.

1951   Erna Fergusson's *New Mexico: A Pageant of Three Peoples* is published. Witter Bynner publishes *Journey With Genius*, describing travels in Mexico with D. H. and Frieda Lawrence.

1957   The Santa Fe Opera opens.

1959   Peggy Pond Church's *The House at Otowi Bridge* is published.

1961   Ancient City Press is launched by Robert Kadlec with the publication of *La Casa Adobe*, by architect William Lumpkins, making it one of Santa Fe's oldest publishers.

1963   Oliver La Farge dies; a branch of the Santa Fe Public Library is named for him.

1964   Erna Fergusson dies; a branch of the Albuquerque Public
                Library is named for her.

1966   New state capitol, the "Roundhouse," is dedicated in Santa Fe.

1967   New Mexico Land Grant War begins in Tierra Amarilla.

1968   *House Made of Dawn* by N. Scott Momaday is published and
                wins the Pulitzer Prize for Fiction, launching what has been
                called the Native American Literary Renaissance. Richard
                Bradford's *Red Sky at Morning* is published. The State Film
                Commission is established.

1970   *The Blessing Way,* the first of Tony Hillerman's Navajo
                mysteries, is published.

1972   *Bless Me, Ultima,* by Rudolfo Anaya, is published.

1974   *My Penitente Land*, by Fray Angélico Chávez, is published.
                John Nichols' *The Milagro Beanfield War*, part of a trilogy, is
                published.

1975   Paul Horgan's *Lamy of Santa Fe* is published; wins the
                Pulitzer Prize for History.

1977   Santa Fe imposes a 3 percent Lodger's Tax to promote
                Santa Fe as "the City Different" to visitors worldwide.
                Marc Simmons' "Trail Dust" column is launched; still runs
                weekly in the *Santa Fe New Mexican.* Leslie Marmon Silko's
                Ceremony is published.

1979   Award-winning poet Jimmy Santiago Baca (now a resident of
                Albuquerque) publishes his first poems in the same year that
                he is released from prison, where he learned to read and write.

1979   Santa Fe Gallery Association formed; Santa Fe has ninety
                art galleries.

1981   The national news media "discovers" Santa Fe, with *Esquire*
                magazine identifying it as "the place to be" and *The Today
                Show* featuring it.

1989   *The Lore of New Mexico*, by Marta Weigle and Peter White,
                receives the Ralph Emerson Twitchell Award for "a
                significant contribution to the field of history" from the
                Historical Society of New Mexico.

1990   Santa Fe reportedly ranks third in the nation's art markets, behind Los Angeles and New York; city now boasts some two hundred art galleries; U.S. Census reports Santa Fe's population as 55,859, with 98,928 in the county.

1991   Tony Hillerman is awarded the Grand Master Award by the Mystery Writers of America for his body of work; he previously won the organization's Edgar Award in 1974.

1992   PEN New Mexico is founded, the largest professional association of writers, editors, and translators in the American Southwest, with headquarters in Santa Fe.

1995   Paul Horgan, professor emeritus and writer-in-residence at Wesleyan University, dies in Middletown, Connecticut; he twice won the Pulitzer Prize for History. Frank Waters dies; he was nominated numerous times for the Nobel Prize in Literature and authored more than twenty books.

1996   Fray Angélico Chávez dies; the History Library of the Palace of the Governors is named in his honor. Michael McGarrity's first crime novel, *Tularosa*, is published.

1997   The Lannan Foundation (supporting artists and writers) moves its headquarters to Santa Fe; soon after, the *Reading and Conversations* lecture series begins, with writers of international stature coming to Santa Fe to participate.

1998   New Mexico celebrates its cuartocentenario, commemorating its 1598 founding by Don Juan de Oñate.

2002   Rudolfo Anaya receives the National Medal of Arts for "exceptional contribution to contemporary American literature that has brought national recognition to the traditions of the Chicano people, and for his efforts to promote Hispanic writers." Richard Bradford dies.

2006   Santa Fe's City Council names Arthur Sze as first poet laureate of the city.

(Sources: *The New Mexico Blue Book* [2005–2006], *The Santa Fe New Mexican's Chronology* [July 1999], and historychannel.com)

Taos Literary Landmarks

THE ARTS ARE THRIVING in Taos today, building on centuries of talent and cultural traditions. Anchored by the monumental Taos Pueblo, the Village of Taos attracts thousands of visitors each year to experience its world-class art, colorful history, and great skiing—all set amidst breathtaking landscapes.

The literary legacy of the Artists and Writers Colonies of the '20s and '30s is strong in Taos today, with numerous acclaimed writers still living there. **John Nichols**, whose New Mexico trilogy includes the popular *The Milagro Beanfield War* (1974), is among the better known writers in Taos today.

The late **Frank Waters** (1902–1995) is legendary in Taos, where he had a part-time home for much of his life. Waters was nominated numerous times for the Nobel Prize in Literature and authored more than twenty books, including *The Man Who Killed the Deer* (1942) and *Masked Gods: Navaho and Pueblo Ceremonialism* (1950).

The Frank Waters Foundation in Taos offers writers' retreats and an artists-in-residence program.

> PO Box 1127
> Taos, NM 87571
> 505/776-2356
> www.frankwaters.org

Mabel Dodge Luhan came to Taos in 1916. She came to the Southwest seeking change, according to the text on the Web site of the Mabel Dodge Luhan House. "Mabel was 'the most common denominator that society, literature, art and radical revolutionaries ever found in New York and Europe.' So claimed a Chicago newspaper reporter in the 1920s of Mabel Dodge Luhan, a woman who attracted leading intellectual and literary figures to her circle for more than four decades. . . . Luhan found her final and best loved home in Taos. Here she married a Taos Pueblo man, Tony Luhan, and set out to establish Taos as the birthplace of a newfound Eden. She brought writers like D. H. Lawrence and Willa Cather, painters like Georgia O'Keeffe and John Marin, and activists like John Collier to help her celebrate and preserve it.

"Mabel and her husband Tony started construction of the 'Big House' in the 1920s, enlarging the 160-year-old home to its present size. The 22-room house is sequestered behind an adobe wall whose gates are ancient altar pieces. . . . The home is registered as a New Mexico state historical site and is listed on the National Register of Historic Places."

The house is available as a conference center, offering workshops on writing, painting, the creative process, and the healing arts.

The Mabel Dodge Luhan House
240 Morada Lane
Taos, NM 87571
505/751-9686 or 800/846-2235
www.mabeldodgeluhan.com

The **D. H. Lawrence Ranch** at San Cristobal, New Mexico (seventeen miles north of Taos), is now a private facility of the University of New Mexico and is often used as a writer's retreat. Both D. H. and Frieda Lawrence are buried at the Kiowa Ranch (their name for it) that Mabel Dodge Luhan gave them in exchange for the original manuscript of *Sons and Lovers*. The facility is open daily; no admission.

505/776-2245.

Another Taos literary landmark is **Moby Dickens Bookshop**, located at 124A Bent Street (#6 Dunn House), near the Taos Plaza. Owner Arthur Bachrach is famous for his knowledge of Southwest literature, and the selection he offers is impressive.

www.mobydickens.com
505/758-3050 or 888/442-9980 toll-free

The newest literary landmark in Taos is the statue of **Padre Antonio José Martínez** (1793–1867), installed in the summer of 2006 on the Taos Plaza. (Padre Martínez was discussed in the Downtown Santa Fe Walk.) He printed the first book in New Mexico Territory, a spelling primer. Padre Martínez is revered in Taos as an outspoken champion of New Mexico's traditional Roman Catholic practices; his resistance to the European influence of Jean Baptiste Lamy, the new bishop, led Lamy to excommunicate Martínez.

Publishers, Booksellers, and Literary Resources

cg

Selected Publishers and Literary Resources

AZRO PRESS

Publishes illustrated children's books with a Southwestern flavor.

> Gae E. Eisenhardt, owner-publisher
> PMB 342
> 1704 Llano Street B
> Santa Fe, NM 87505
> 505/989-3272
> www.azropress.com

BORDER BOOK FESTIVAL

Annual gathering of writers, publishers, and booksellers.

> Denise Chávez, artistic director
> 430 La Colonia Street
> Las Cruces, NM 88005
> 505/524-1499

CLEAR LIGHT PUBLISHERS

Publishes Native American and Western titles focusing on art, culture, and traditional lifestyles, including biography, children's books, cookbooks, and history.

> Harmon Houghton and Marcia Keegan, owners-publishers
> 823 Don Diego Avenue
> Santa Fe, NM 87505
> 505/989-9590 or 800/253-2747 toll-free
> www.clearlightbooks.com

DOROTHY DOYLE'S READING SAMPLER

Doyle is a journalist and novelist who produces "The Reading Sampler," KSFR 90.7 FM, Santa Fe Public Radio's weekly review of books.

GIBBS SMITH, PUBLISHER

A leading publisher of lifestyle books since 1969, Gibbs Smith, Publisher (GSP), acquired Santa Fe–based Ancient City Press (ACP) in 2005. The ACP imprint was discontinued in 2007, but GSP continues its tradition of producing fine illustrated books on Southwestern culture, art, history, and cuisine.

> www.gibbs-smith.com
>
> 801/544-9800 or 800/748-5439 toll-free

JOE HAYES, STORYTELLER

Joe Hayes is well known in Santa Fe as the man who tells the stories every summer near the tipi at the Wheelwright Museum. The author of many books, Hayes spins tales of Southwest lore, Native American legend, and Spanish stories (*cuentos*). He appears outdoors on weekends in July and August at the following address:

> Wheelwright Museum of the American Indian
>
> 704 Camino Lejo
>
> Santa Fe, NM 87505
>
> 505/982-4636 or 800/607-4636 toll-free
>
> www.wheelwright.org

LANNAN FOUNDATION

The Lannan Foundation is dedicated to cultural freedom, diversity, and creativity through projects that support exceptional contemporary artists and writers as well as inspired native activists in rural indigenous communities.

> 313 Read Street
>
> Santa Fe, NM 87501
>
> 505/986-8160
>
> www.lannan.org.

The foundation sponsors the prestigious *Readings & Conversations* series, featuring noted authors from around the world reading their work, followed by on-stage conversation. These readings are held at the Lensic Performing Arts Center:

> 211 West San Francisco Street
>
> 505/988-1234
>
> www.lensic.com

LITERACY VOLUNTEERS OF SANTA FE

As a recognized literacy leader in northern New Mexico, Literacy Volunteers of Santa Fe has provided instruction to more than 8,500 students, with 97 percent coming from low-income households. Free services include one-to-one basic literacy instruction for adults, workplace tutoring, and English language learner teams.

> 6401 Richards Avenue
> Santa Fe, NM 87508
> 505/428-1353
> www.lvsf.org

MUSEUM OF NEW MEXICO PRESS

Produces fine books on the arts, anthropology, architecture, and cultural traditions of New Mexico and the Southwest.

> Anna Gallegos, director
> 725 Camino Lejo
> 505/476-1154
> Santa Fe, NM 87505
> www.mnmpress.org

NEW MEXICO BOOK ASSOCIATION

Founded in 1994, this is a group for book professionals (publishers, editors, writers, printers, librarians, agents, production houses, publicists, and marketing people).

> PO Box 1285
> Santa Fe, NM 87504
> 505/983-1412
> www.nmbook.org

OCEAN TREE BOOKS

Quality trade books since 1983; publishes travel guidebooks, peacemaking guides, and Legacy Editions.

> Richard Polese, owner-publisher
> PO Box 1295
> 505/983-1412
> Santa Fe, NM 87504
> www.oceantree.com

PEN NEW MEXICO

This is the local chapter of PEN USA. PEN-NM was founded in 1992, and is the largest association of writers in the Southwest. A worldwide writers' organization, PEN International was founded in 1922 to promote friendship and intellectual cooperation among writers everywhere. Through its Freedom to Write Committee, PEN New Mexico has campaigned for the release of imprisoned writers and has established a Santa Fe/Albuquerque asylum zone within the Network of North American Cities of Asylum.

> 505/920-2357

RECURSOS DE SANTA FE

Sponsors writers' conferences and readings organized by the Southwest Literary Center.

> Ellen Bradbury-Reid, executive director
> 826 Camino del Monte Rey, A3
> Santa Fe, NM 87505
> 505/982-9301
> www.recursos.org

SAR PRESS (SCHOOL OF AMERICAN RESEARCH)

Long respected for exceptional editorial, design, and production standards, the SAR Press aids the School of American Research in achieving its mission to communicate the insights of anthropology and related disciplines to both popular and scholarly audiences. In 2007 the press will launch a dynamic, interactive, online learning matrix for secondary school teachers and students. *Southwest Crossroads: Cultures and Histories of the American Southwest* will offer original texts, maps, images, oral histories, and films, providing teaching and curriculum materials for grades seven through twelve.

> PO Box 2188
> Santa Fe, NM 87504
> 505/954-7206 or 888/390-6070
> www.press.sarweb.org

St. John's College, Santa Fe
The tradition of St. John's College is the tutorial method and reading original texts—some call it the Great Books curriculum. The original St. John's College, located in Annapolis, Maryland, is the nation's third oldest institution of higher learning. The Santa Fe campus opened in 1964 and has a graduate institute along with its liberal arts undergraduate program. Studies in the Eastern classics are offered, as well as a Summer Classics in Santa Fe program that features classic literature and the Santa Fe Opera. St. John's Library and Fine Arts Guild brings community members together to celebrate literature and the fine arts. The Santa Fe community also participates in lectures, seminars, and musical concerts year-round.

> 1160 Camino Cruz Blanca
> Santa Fe, NM 87505
> 505/984-6000
> www.stjohnscollege.edu

Sunstone Press
Has been engaged in independent publishing since 1971; Southwest Heritage Series reprints vintage and out-of-print Southwest classics.

> James Clois Smith, owner-publisher
> PO Box 2321
> Santa Fe, NM 87504
> 800/243-5644 toll-free
> www.sunstonepress.com

University of New Mexico Press
Publishes wide range of Southwest literature.

> Luther Wilson, director
> 1312 Basehart Road SE
> Albuquerque, NM 87106
> 505/277-2346
> www.unmpress.com

Western Edge Press/Sherman Asher Publishing
Publishes Southwest books and offers book project management, design, and production services; color reproduction specialist.

Jim Mafchir
126 Candelario Street
Santa Fe, NM 87501
505/988-7214
www.shermanasher.com

WordHarvest Writers Workshops

One-day workshops year-round; a variety of topics are presented by published authors.

Anne Hillerman
304 Calle Oso
Santa Fe, NM 87501
505/471-1565
www.wordharvest.com

Newspapers and Periodicals

El Palacio

The quarterly magazine of the Museum of New Mexico, *El Palacio* features articles on museum exhibitions and behind-the-scenes reporting on museum events and collections, along with member news and previews. It was established in 1913 and is sold on newsstands as well as by subscription (a benefit of membership in the Museum of New Mexico Foundation).

Debora Bluestone, managing editor
Museum Services
PO Box 2087
Santa Fe, NM 87504
www.elpalacio.org

La Herencia

A regional magazine, *La Herencia* is known as the voice of Hispanic culture in the Southwest. Founded in 1994, the magazine published its fiftieth issue in the summer of 2006. Its parent company, Gran Via Publications, also publishes books on Southwestern Hispanic culture.

Ana Pacheco, editor and publisher
PO Box 22576
Santa Fe, NM 87502
www.herencia.com

NEW MEXICO MAGAZINE

The nation's first state magazine, *New Mexico Magazine* is published monthly by the New Mexico Tourism Department. It dates from 1912, and during its history, most of New Mexico's leading writers and photographers have contributed to it on a regular basis.

Emily Drabanski, editor in chief
Lew Wallace Building
495 Old Santa Fe Trail
Santa Fe, NM 87501
www.nmmagazine.com

SANTA FEAN MAGAZINE

The magazine for the City Different, the *Santa Fean* is published monthly (except January/February) by Southwest Media, LLC. It is an award-winning lifestyle publication with emphasis on the arts and culture of Santa Fe and northern New Mexico.

Southwest Media, LLC
Ashleigh Morris, editor in chief
466 West San Francisco Street
Santa Fe, NM 87501
505/983-1444
www.santafean.com

THE SANTA FE NEW MEXICAN

The West's oldest newspaper, the *Santa Fe New Mexican,* founded in 1849, publishes daily, with various magazine supplements throughout the year. Its weekly arts-and-entertainment supplement, *Pasatiempo,* has won numerous awards for its design and content.

Robin M. Martin, editor and publisher

202 East Marcy Street

Santa Fe, NM 87501

www.freenewmexican.com

SANTA FE REPORTER

Santa Fe's alternative, free weekly newspaper, the *Santa Fe Reporter,* is known for sound investigative reporting and an imaginative approach to covering local arts and entertainment. It has been doing its job for the community since 1974.

Andy Dudzik, publisher

Julia Goldberg, editor

132 East Marcy Street

Santa Fe, NM 87501

505/985-5541

www.sfreporter.com

Selected Booksellers and Specialty Businesses

★ Bookstores with cats in residence

ALLÁ: LIBROS, ARTE, MÚSICA

Jim Dunlap's Allá Bookstore, reputed to be the largest Spanish-language bookstore in the United States, is a Santa Fe "institution." Open Monday through Saturday, 12:00 noon to 6:00 p.m.

102 West San Francisco Street (up one level)

Santa Fe, NM 87501

505/988-5416

COLLECTED WORKS BOOKSTORE ★

Since 1978, the bookstore has specialized in books about New Mexico and the Southwest, including fiction, art, architecture, children's books, and cookbooks. Hosts many author readings, local and national, as well as writers' groups and book clubs.

Dorothy Massey, owner (and guardian of Kitty Carson, resident cat)

208-B West San Francisco Street

Santa Fe, NM 87501

505/988-4226 or 877/988-4226 toll-free

www.collectedworksbookstore.com

Dumont Maps & Books of the West ★

Offers antique maps, out-of-print and rare books, prints, and ephemera, specializing in the American West; catalogs issued regularly and online. Located around the corner from the Georgia O'Keeffe Museum.

Andre and Carol Dumont, owners

(and guardians of Mr. Murphy, resident cat)

314 McKenzie Street

Santa Fe, NM 87501

505/988-1076

www.dumontbooks.com

Garcia Street Books

This is a fine independent bookstore that is popular with locals. It showcases local authors as well as many of the nation's most respected writers, and presents book exhibitions.

Edward and Eva Borins, owners

376 Garcia Street

Santa Fe, NM 87501

505/986-0151 or 866/986-0151 toll-free

www.garciastreetbooks.com

Gunstock Hill Books

Rare and used books, Western Americana, antique bookends.

Henry Lewis, owner

142 Daniel Street

Santa Fe, NM 87501

505/983-0088

NICHOLAS POTTER BOOKSELLER

This is Santa Fe's oldest bookstore for used and collectible books. Nick Potter is a second-generation Santa Fe bookseller dealing in general used and out-of-print books, including a good selection of Southwest literature; also CDs (classical and jazz).

> 211 East Palace Avenue
> Santa Fe, NM 87501
> 505/983-5434

TRAVEL BUG COFFEE SHOP

Specializing in travel books, guides, maps, USGS maps, and travel accessories; section on Santa Fe and the Southwest; hosts author presentations and readings.

> 839 Paseo de Peralta
> Santa Fe, NM 87501
> 505/992-0418 or 866-992-0418 toll free
> www.mapsofnewmexico.com

TRUE BELIEVERS COMICS & GALLERY

Specializes in original comic art, DVD rentals, special orders, and thousands of comics old and new.

> 435 South Guadalupe Street
> Santa Fe, NM 87501
> 505/992-TRUE (8783)

VIDEO LIBRARY INC.

Santa Fe's most popular place for vintage and current VHS-DVD rentals since 1981; provides major new releases, international cinema, cult and art house films; has a special section of films made in New Mexico.

> Lisa Harris, owner-operator
> 120 East Marcy Street #1
> Santa Fe, NM 87501
> 505/983-3321

Writers' Workshops, Conferences, and Retreats

ය

In Santa Fe

SANTA FE FILM FESTIVAL

The annual Santa Fe Film Festival has been held in early December since 2000, attracting independent filmmakers and established industry leaders nationwide. The Festival screens new and vintage films and also honors industry notables through its Luminaria Awards. Related to the Festival, the New Mexico Film Office organized the first annual New Mexico Filmmakers Conference in December 2006 to help link filmmakers across the state. The two-day conference held in Santa Fe featured practical hands-on workshops and seminars.

> www.santafefilmfestival.com
> 505/988-5225;
> www.nmfilm.com
> 505/827-9810 or 800/545-9871 toll-free

SANTA FE SHORT STORY FESTIVAL

The second annual festival was held in the summer of 2006; plans are for this festival to continue each year. Authors such as Joyce Carol Oates, Edna O'Brien, Tony Hillerman, N. Scott Momaday, and Rudolfo Anaya have participated in the first two Festivals.

> www.santafeshortstory.org
> 505/466-3440

SANTA FE WRITERS CONFERENCE

The conference is held each summer, with respected authors, local and national, serving on the faculty. A series of evening readings is part of the popular conference that has been sponsored by the **Southwest Literary Center** since 1984. The center is a division of **Recursos de Santa Fe**, a private nonprofit organization that presents nationally recognized seminars and conferences in the arts, sciences, letters, and humanities.

> www.santafewritersconference.com
> 505/577-1125

WORDHARVEST WRITERS WORKSHOPS

The workshops are held year-round on a range of topics, with local and regional authors presenting. All workshops are limited to 15 participants and are held in a writer's home near the Santa Fe Plaza. WordHarvest also sponsors the Tony Hillerman Writers Conference—Focus on Mystery, which has become an annual event, usually held in the fall in Albuquerque, New Mexico.

>   www.wordharvest.com
>   505/471-1565

In Taos

MABEL DODGE LUHAN HOUSE

This facility continues to present workshops for writers and painters throughout the year.

>   www.mabeldodgeluhan.com
>   505/751-9686 or
>   800/846-2235 toll-free

FRANK WATERS FOUNDATION

The foundation offers writers' retreats and an artists-in-residence program.

>   www.frankwaters.org
>   505/776-2356

TAOS SUMMER WRITERS' CONFERENCE

The conference is presented by the University of New Mexico, which now operates the D. H. Lawrence Ranch, just north of Taos. The Taos Summer Writers' Conference is held in July each year, a week filled with workshops, cultural events, readings, and presentations. For a fee, participants may also schedule a consultation with one of the visiting agents or editors.

>   www.unm.edu/~taosconf
>   505/277-5572

S.O.M.O.S. (THE SOCIETY OF THE MUSE OF THE SOUTHWEST)

The society supports and nurtures the literary arts, in both written and oral traditions, honoring cultural diversity in the Southwest. Summer workshops are offered.

>   www.somostaos.org
>   505/758-0081 or 877/758-7343 toll-free

New Mexico Literary Classics
and Other Recommended Books

☙

Fiction

Abbey, Edward. *The Brave Cowboy.* New York: Harper Perennial (division of HarperCollins Publishers), 1992.

Anaya, Rudolfo. *Bless Me, Ultima.* New York: Warner Books, 1994.

———. *Serafina's Stories.* Albuquerque: University of New Mexico Press, 2004.

Austin, Mary. *Starry Adventure.* Boston: Houghton Mifflin, 1931.

Bandelier, Adolph. *The Delight Makers.* New York: Dodd Publishing, 1890.

Bradford, Richard. *Red Sky at Morning.* New York: Perennial Classics, Harper Perennial (division HarperCollins Publishers), 1999.

———. *So Far From Heaven.* Philadelphia, PA: Lippincott Williams & Wilkins, 1973.

Cather, Willa. *Death Comes for the Archbishop.* Vintage Classics ed. New York: Random House, 1990.

Chávez, Denise. *Loving Pedro Infante: A Novel.* New York: Washington Square Press (an imprint of Simon and Schuster), 2001.

Fergusson, Harvey. *The Conquest of Don Pedro.* New York: William Morrow & Co., 1954.

———. *Grant of Kingdom.* New York: William Morrow & Co., 1950.

Hamilton, Donald. *Death of a Citizen.* New York: Fawcett (an imprint of Random House), 1984.

Hillerman, Tony. Selected titles: *The Blessing Way, People of Darkness, Skinwalkers, A Thief of Time, Coyote Waits.* New York: HarperCollins Publishers.

Hughes, Dorothy B. *Ride the Pink Horse.* Reprint ed. New York: Carroll & Graf Publishers (an imprint of Avalon Publishing Group), 1988.

La Farge, Oliver. *Laughing Boy: A Navajo Love Story.* Boston: Houghton Mifflin Co., 1929.

Laughlin, Ruth. *The Wind Leaves No Shadow*. Caldwell, ID: Caxton Printers, Ltd., 1951.

Lovett, Sarah. *A Desperate Silence: A Dr. Sylvia Strange Novel*. New York: Villard (an imprint of Random House), 1998.

McGarrity, Michael. *Nothing But Trouble: A Kevin Kerney Novel*. New York: Dutton, 2005.

————. *Tularosa*. Reprint ed. New York: Pocket Star (an imprint of Simon & Schuster), 1997.

Momaday, N. Scott. *House Made of Dawn*. New York: HarperCollins Publishers, 1968.

————. *The Way to Rainy Mountain*. Reprint ed. Albuquerque: University of New Mexico Press, 1977.

Nichols, John. *The Milagro Beanfield War*. New York: Holt, Rinehart and Winston, 1974.

Richter, Conrad. *The Sea of Grass.* New York: Knopf, 1937.

Rhodes, Eugene Manlove. *Pasó por Aquí*. Norman: University of Oklahoma Press, 1973.

Silko, Leslie Marmon. *Ceremony*. Reprint ed. New York: Penguin Books, 1986.

Waters, Frank. *The Man Who Killed the Deer*. New York: Farrar, Straus and Giroux, 1942.

————. *People of the Valley*. Athens, OH: Swallow Press (a division of Ohio University Press), 1969.

Zollinger, Norman. *Riders to Cibola*. New York: A Forge Book published by Tom Doherty Associates, Inc., 1995.

Nonfiction

Austin, Mary. *The Land of Journeys' Ending*. Tucson: University of Arizona Press, 1983 reissue.

Caffey, David L. *Land Of Enchantment, Land Of Conflict: New Mexico In English Language Fiction*. College Station: Texas A&M University Press, 1999.

Chávez, Fray Angélico. *My Penitente Land: Reflections on Spanish New Mexico*. Albuquerque: University of New Mexico Press, 1974.

Chávez, Fray Angélico. *Origins of New Mexico Families: A Genealogy of the Spanish Colonial Period.* Revised ed. Santa Fe: Museum of New Mexico Press, 1992.

Church, Peggy Pond. *The House at Otowi Bridge: The Story of Edith Warner and Los Alamos.* Albuquerque: University of New Mexico Press, 1959.

DeBuys, William. *Enchantment and Exploitation: The Life and Hard Times of a New Mexico Mountain Range.* Albuquerque: University of New Mexico Press, 1985.

Dunaway, David King, and Sara L. Spurgeon. *Writing the Southwest.* New York: Plume (an imprint of Dutton Signet, a division of Penguin Books), 1995.

Johnson, George. *Fire in the Mind: Science, Faith, and the Search for Order.* New York: Vintage (a division of Random House), 1996.

Lummis, Charles F. *The Land of Poco Tiempo.* Albuquerque: University of New Mexico Press, 1952.

Miller, Jay. *Billy the Kid Rides Again: Digging for the Truth.* Santa Fe: Sunstone Press, 2005.

Wallis, Michael, ed. *En Divina Luz: The Penitente Moradas of New Mexico.* Albuquerque: University of New Mexico Press, 1994.

Weigle, Marta, ed. *Brothers of Light, Brothers of Blood: The Penitentes of the Southwest.* Santa Fe: Ancient City Press, 1976.

Wilson, Chris. *The Myth of Santa Fe: The Creation of a Modern Regional Tradition.* Albuquerque: University of New Mexico Press, 1997.

Biography and History

Baca, Elmo. *Mabel's Santa Fe and Taos: Bohemian Legends, 1900–1950.* Salt Lake City: Gibbs Smith, Publisher, 2000.

Bryan, Howard. *Incredible Elfego Baca: Good Man, Bad Man of the Old West.* Santa Fe: Clear Light Books, 1993.

Cabeza de Vaca, Fabiola. *We Fed Them Cactus.* Albuquerque: University of New Mexico Press, 1954.

Chávez, Fray Angélico. *But Time and Chance: The Story of Padre Martínez of Taos, 1793–1867.* Santa Fe: Sunstone Press, 1981.

Chávez, Thomas E. *An Illustrated History of New Mexico*. Albuquerque: University of New Mexico Press, 2002.

Conant, Jennet. *109 East Palace: Robert Oppenheimer and the Secret City of Los Alamos*. New York: Simon & Schuster, 2005.

Cook, Mary Straw. *Loretto: The Sisters and Their Santa Fe Chapel*. Santa Fe: Museum of New Mexico Press, 2002.

Díaz del Castillo, Bernal. *The Discovery and Conquest of Mexico, 1517–1521*. Ed. by Genaro García. Trans. by A. P. Maudslay. New York: Farrar, Straus and Giroux, 1956.

Dye, Victoria E. *All Aboard for Santa Fe: Railway Promotion of the Southwest, 1890s to 1930s*. Albuquerque: University of New Mexico Press, 2005.

Ebright, Malcolm, and Rick Hendricks. *The Witches of Abiquiu: The Governor, the Priest, the Genízaro Indians, and the Devil*. Albuquerque: University of New Mexico Press, 2006.

Fergusson, Erna. *New Mexico: A Pageant of Three Peoples*. Reprint ed. Albuquerque: University of New Mexico Press, 1980.

Folsom, Franklin. *Indian Uprising on the Rio Grande: The Pueblo Revolt of 1680*. Albuquerque: University of New Mexico Press, 1996.

Gish, Robert Franklin. *Beautiful Swift Fox: Erna Fergusson and the Modern Southwest*. College Station: Texas A&M University Press, 1996.

Gish, Robert Franklin. *Frontier's End: The Life and Literature of Harvey Fergusson*. Lincoln: University of Nebraska Press, 1988.

Gregg, Josiah. *Commerce of the Prairies*. Reprint ed. Norman: University of Oklahoma Press, 1990.

Gutiérrez, Ramón A. *When Jesus Came the Corn Mothers Went Away: Marriage, Sexuality and Power in New Mexico, 1500–1846*. Palo Alto: Stanford University Press, 1991.

Horgan, Paul. *The Centuries of Santa Fe*. Santa Fe: William Gannon, 1976.

———. *Great River: The Rio Grande in North American History* (2 vols. in one). 4th Reprint ed. Middletown, CT: Wesleyan University Press, 1991.

———. *Lamy of Santa Fe: His Life and Times*. New York: Farrar, Straus and Giroux, 1975.

Jenkins, Myra Ellen and Albert H. Schroeder. *A Brief History of New Mexico*. Albuquerque: University of New Mexico Press, 1993.

Kraft, James. *Who Is Witter Bynner? A Biography*. Albuquerque: University of New Mexico Press, 1995.

La Farge, John Pen. *Turn Left at the Sleeping Dog: Scripting the Santa Fe Legend, 1920–1955*. Albuquerque: University of New Mexico Press, 2001.

La Farge, Oliver, with Arthur N. Morgan. *Santa Fe: The Autobiography of a Southwestern Town*. Norman: University of Oklahoma Press, 1959.

Nolan, Frederick W. *The West of Billy the Kid*. Norman: University of Oklahoma Press, 1999.

Pearce, T. M. *Mary Hunter Austin*. New York: MacMillan Publishing Company, 1984.

Poling-Kempes, Lesley. *The Harvey Girls: Women Who Opened the West*. Reprint ed. Tucson, AZ: Treasure Chest Books, 1991.

Rudnick, Lois Palken. *Mabel Dodge Luhan: New Woman, New Worlds*. Albuquerque: University of New Mexico Press, 1984.

Sando, Joe. S., and Herman Agoyo, eds. *Po'pay: Leader of the First American Revolution*. Santa Fe: Clear Light Publishing, 2005.

Sides, Hampton. *Blood and Thunder: An Epic of the American West*. New York: Doubleday, 2006.

———. *Ghost Soldiers: The Epic Account of World War II's Greatest Rescue Mission*. New York: Random House, 2001.

Simmons, Marc. *New Mexico Mavericks: Stories from a Fabled Past*. Santa Fe: Sunstone Press, 2005.

Smith, Pamela S., with Richard Polese. *Passions in Print: Private Press Artistry in New Mexico, 1834–Present*. Santa Fe: Museum of New Mexico Press, 2006.

Udall, Sharyn R. *Spud Johnson & Laughing Horse*. Albuquerque: University of New Mexico Press, 1994.

Udall, Stewart. *In Coronado's Footsteps*. Tucson, AZ: Southwest Parks and Monuments Association, 1991.

Weigle, Marta, and Kyle Fiore. *Santa Fe & Taos: The Writer's Era, 1916–1941*. Santa Fe: Ancient City Press, 1982.

Memoirs, Journals, Essays, Poetry, and Belles Lettres

Bynner, Witter. *Journey with Genius: Recollections and Reflections Concerning the D. H. Lawrences.* New York: John Day Company, 1951.

Cleaveland, Agnes Morley. *No Life for a Lady.* Women of the West series. Lincoln: University of Nebraska Press, 1977.

Henderson, Alice Corbin. *Red Earth: Poems of New Mexico.* Reissue ed. Comp. and ed. by Lois P. Rudnick and Ellen Zieselman. Santa Fe: Museum of New Mexico Press, 2003.

Hillerman, Tony. *The Great Taos Bank Robbery and Other Indian Country Affairs.* Albuquerque: University of New Mexico Press, 1973.

———, ed. *The Spell of New Mexico.* Albuquerque: University of New Mexico Press, 1976.

Kraft, James, ed. *The Selected Witter Bynner.* Albuquerque: University of New Mexico Press, 1995.

La Farge, Oliver. *Behind the Mountains.* North Hollywood, CA: Charles Publishing Company, 1994.

Luhan, Mabel Dodge. *Winter In Taos.* Denver, CO: Sage Books, 1935.

Magoffin, Susan Shelby. *Down the Santa Fe Trail and into Mexico: The Diary of Susan Shelby Magoffin, 1846–1847.* Ed. by Stella M. Drumm. Lincoln: University of Nebraska Press, 1982.

McCord, Richard. *The Other State: New Mexico, USA.* Santa Fe: Sunstone Press, 2003.

Momaday, N. Scott. *The Names: A Memoir.* Reprint ed. Tucson: University of Arizona Press, 1987.

Niederman, Sharon, and Miriam Sagan, eds. *New Mexico Poetry Renaissance.* Santa Fe: Red Crane Books, 1994.

Russell, Marian Sloan. *Land of Enchantment: Memoirs of Marian Russell Along the Santa Fe Trail: As Dictated to Mrs. Hal Russell.* Reprint ed. Albuquerque: University of New Mexico Press, 1985.

Russell, Sharman Apt. *Songs of the Flute Player: Seasons of Life in the Southwest.* New York: Perseus Books, 1991.

Waters, Frank. *Of Time and Change.* Denver, CO: MacMurray & Beck, Inc., 1998.

Folklore and Culture

Applegate, Frank. *Native Tales of New Mexico.* Philadelphia: J.B. Lippincott Co., 1932.

Aranda, Charles. *Dichos: Proverbs and Sayings from the Spanish.* Santa Fe: Sunstone Press, 1977.

Cobos, Rubén. *Refranes: Southwestern Spanish Proverbs.* Santa Fe: Museum of New Mexico Press, 1985.

Crawford, Stanley G. *Mayordomo: Chronicle of an Acequia in Northern New Mexico.* Reprint ed. Albuquerque: University of New Mexico Press, 1993.

Erdoes, Richard, and Alfonso Ortiz, eds. *American Indian Myths and Legends.* New York: Pantheon Books, 1984.

Fergusson, Erna. *Dancing Gods: Indian Ceremonials of New Mexico and Arizona.* Reprint ed. Albuquerque: University of New Mexico Press, 1970.

García, Nasario, ed. *Brujas, Bultos, y Brasas: Tales of Witchcraft and the Supernatural in the Pecos Valley.* Santa Fe: Western Edge Press, 1999.

Griego y Maestas, José, and Rudolfo Anaya. *Cuentos: Tales from the Hispanic Southwest.* Santa Fe: Museum of New Mexico Press, 1980.

La Farge, Oliver. *The Mother Ditch (La Acequia Madre).* Santa Fe: Sunstone Press, 1983.

Velarde, Pablita. *Old Father Story Teller.* Santa Fe: Clear Light Publishers, 1989.

Waters, Frank. *Masked Gods: Navaho and Pueblo Ceremonialism.* 2nd ed. Athens, OH: Swallow Press, 1950.

Weigle, Marta, and Peter White. *The Lore of New Mexico.* Albuquerque: University of New Mexico Press, 1988.

Children's and Young Adult Books

Anaya, Rudolfo. *The Farolitos of Christmas.* New York: Hyperion, 1995.

Carson, William C. *Peter Becomes a Trail Man: The Story of a Boy's Journey on the Santa Fe Trail.* Albuquerque: University of New Mexico Press, 2002.

Dewey, Jennifer Owings. *Stories on Stone, Rock Art: Images from the Ancient Ones*. Albuquerque: University of New Mexico Press, 2003.

Hillerman, Tony. *The Boy Who Made Dragonfly: A Zuni Myth*. Albuquerque: University of New Mexico Press, 1986.

Krumgold, Joseph. *And Now, Miguel*. Reissue ed. New York: HarperTrophy, 1984.

Momaday, N. Scott. *Circle of Wonder: A Native American Christmas Story*. Albuquerque: University of New Mexico Press, 1999.

Mora, Pat. *Maria Paints the Hills*. Santa Fe: Museum of New Mexico Press, 2002.

Murphy, Barbara Beasley. *Miguel Lost & Found in the Palace*. Santa Fe: Museum of New Mexico Press, 2002.

Ortega, Cristina. *The Eyes of the Weaver (Los Ojos del Tejedor)*. Albuquerque: University of New Mexico Press, 2006.

Ortiz, Simon J. *The Good Rainbow Road (Rawa 'Kashtyaa' Tsi Hiyaani)*. Tucson: University of Arizona Press, 2004.

Sagel, Jim. *A Garden Of Stories (Jardín de Cuentos)*. Santa Fe: Red Crane Books, 1996.

Simmons, Marc. *José's Buffalo Hunt—A Story from History. Children of the West series*. Albuquerque: University of New Mexico Press, 2003.

Velarde, Pablita. *Old Father Story Teller*. Santa Fe: Clear Light Publishers, 1989.

Warm Day, Jonathan. *Taos Pueblo Painted Stories*. Santa Fe: Clear Light Publishers, 2004.

References

Cobos, Rubén. *Dictionary of New Mexico and Southern Colorado Spanish*. Bilingual ed. Santa Fe: Museum of New Mexico Press, 2003.

Julyan, Robert. *The Place Names of New Mexico*. Albuquerque: University of New Mexico Press, 1996.

Work Projects Administration. *The WPA Guide to 1930s New Mexico*. Tucson: University of Arizona Press, 1989.

WPA Federal Writers Project. *New Mexico: A Guide to the Colorful State*. New York: Hastings House, 1940.

Bibliography

Books

Bradford, Richard. *Red Sky at Morning.* Perennial Classics ed. New York: Harper Perennial (division HarperCollins Publishers), 1999.

Cather, Willa. *Death Comes for the Archbishop.* Vintage Classics ed. New York: Random House, 1990.

Chávez, Fray Angélico. *My Penitente Land: Reflections on Spanish New Mexico.* Albuquerque: University of New Mexico Press, 1974.

Church, Peggy Pond. *The House at Otowi Bridge: The Story of Edith Warner and Los Alamos.* Albuquerque: University of New Mexico Press, 1959, 1960.

Dickinson, Donald C., W. David Laird, and Margaret F. Maxwell, eds. *Voices From the Southwest: A Gathering of Poetry, Essays, and Art in Honor of Lawrence Clark Powell.* Flagstaff, AZ: Northland Press, 1976.

Dobie, J. Frank. *Guide To Life and Literature of the Southwest.* Dallas: Southern Methodist University Press, 1952.

Dunaway, David King, and Sara L. Spurgeon. *Writing the Southwest.* New York: Plume (an imprint of Dutton Signet, a division of Penguin Books), 1995.

Folsom, Franklin. *Indian Uprising on the Rio Grande: The Pueblo Revolt of 1680.* Albuquerque: University of New Mexico Press, 1996.

Fowles, John. *Daniel Martin.* Boston: Little, Brown and Company, 1977.

García, Nasario, ed. *Brujas, Bultos, y Brasas: Tales of Witchcraft and the Supernatural in the Pecos Valley.* Santa Fe: Western Edge Press, 1999.

Gallegos, Bernardo P. *Literacy, Education, and Society in New Mexico, 1693–1821.* Albuquerque: University of New Mexico Press, 1992.

Gish, Robert Franklin. *Beautiful Swift Fox: Erna Fergusson and the Modern Southwest.* College Station: Texas A&M University Press, 1996.

Hemp, Bill. *Taos Landmarks and Legends.* Tucson, AZ: Treasure Chest Books, 1995.

Hillerman, Tony. *The Great Taos Bank Robbery and Other Indian Country Affairs.* Albuquerque: University of New Mexico Press, 1973.

————, ed. *The Spell of New Mexico*. Albuquerque: University of New Mexico Press, 1976.

Historic Santa Fe Foundation, The. *Old Santa Fe Today*. 4th ed. Albuquerque: University of New Mexico Press, 1991.

Horgan, Paul. *The Centuries of Santa Fe*. Santa Fe: William Gannon, 1976.

————. *Lamy of Santa Fe: His Life and Times*. New York: Farrar, Straus and Giroux, 1975.

————. *Tracings: A Book of Partial Portraits*. New York: Farrar Straus Giroux, 1993.

Krause, Martin F. *Gustave Baumann: Nearer to Art*. Santa Fe: Museum of New Mexico Press, 1993.

La Farge, John Pen. *Turn Left at the Sleeping Dog: Scripting the Santa Fe Legend, 1920–1955*. Albuquerque: University of New Mexico Press, 2001.

La Farge, Oliver, with Arthur N. Morgan. *Santa Fe: The Autobiography of a Southwestern Town*. Norman: University of Oklahoma Press, 1959.

Lyon, Thomas J., ed. *A Literary History of the American West*. Fort Worth: Texas Christian University Press, 1986.

Luther, T. N. *Collecting Santa Fe Authors*. Santa Fe: Ancient City Press (an imprint of Gibbs Smith, Publisher), 2002.

Meyer, Marian. *Santa Fe's Fifteen Club: A Century of Literary Women*. Santa Fe: privately published by the author, 1991.

Noble, David Grant, ed. *Santa Fe: History of an Ancient City*. Santa Fe: School of American Research Press, 1989.

Ruoff, A., Lavonne Brown, and Frank W. Porter III, gen. ed. *Literatures of the American Indian*. New York and Philadelphia: Chelsea House Publishers (a division of Main Line Book Co.), 1991.

Simmons, Marc. *New Mexico: An Interpretive History*. Albuquerque: University of New Mexico Press, 1993.

————. *New Mexico Mavericks: Stories from a Fabled Past*. Santa Fe: Sunstone Press, 2005.

van Hulsteyn, Peggy. *Sleeping with Literary Lions: The Booklover's Guide to Bed and Breakfasts*. Golden, CO: Fulcrum Publishing, 1997.

Wallace, Susan E. *The Land of the Pueblos*. New York: John B. Alden, Publisher, 1888.

Weigle, Marta, and Kyle Fiore. *Santa Fe & Taos: The Writer's Era, 1916–1941*. Santa Fe: Ancient City Press, 1982.

————, and Peter White. *The Lore of New Mexico*. Albuquerque: University of New Mexico Press, 1988.

Woods, Betty. *101 Men and Women of New Mexico*. Santa Fe: Sunstone Press, 1976.

Articles

Cohen, Saul. "The 10 Best Novels of New Mexico." *New Mexico Magazine,* March/April 1974.

Davis, William E. "Bud." "A Novel Approach." *New Mexico Magazine,* December 2003.

Powell, Lawrence Clark. "50 Good Books About New Mexico." *New Mexico Magazine,* January 1960.

Smith, Pamela. "The Role of Women in New Mexico's Private Press Movement." *El Palacio,* vol. 3, no. 1.

Other

Lasting Impressions: The Private Presses of New Mexico, a museum exhibition at the Palace of the Governors, February 18, 2005, through February 7, 2007; auxiliary printed materials, online resources, lectures, gallery talks, and presentations at the Fray Angélico Chávez History Library.

Lasting Impressions: A Library Legacy, a related and concurrent exhibition at the New Mexico State Library; lecture series, auxiliary printed materials, including a literary map of New Mexico.

Time Traveler Maps. *Tony Hillerman's Indian Country Map & Guide.* Mancos, CO, 1998.

Image Credits

Abbreviations

MNM/DCA: Photo Archives, Courtesy of Palace of the Governors
NN: negative number

Credits

page ii: Wood engraving: *Street Scene in New Mexico,*
MNM/DCA (NN89210)
page 6: MNM/DCA (NN135044)
page 9: MNM/DCA (NN152680)
page 15: Photo by Carl Sheppard, MNM/DCA (NN130965)
page 17: Detail of a Santa Fe map, 1882, by lithographers Beck &
Pault, MNM/DCA (NN23306)
page 22: MNM/DCA (NN7123)
page 27: Photo by Witter Bynner, MNM/DCA (NN124373)
page 33: Photo by Tyler Dingee, MNM/DCA (NN51310)
page 39: Photo by T. Harmon Parkhurst, MNM/DCA (NN54310)
page 40: MNM/DCA (NN46940)
page 41: Photo by Tyler Dingee, MNM/DCA (NN120361)
page 43: Photo by Will Connell, MNM/DCA (NN59764)
page 45: MNM/DCA (NN51700)
page 47: Photo by Barbara J. Harrelson
page 51: Photo by T. Harmon Parkhurst, MNM/DCA (NN51395)
page 56: Wood engraving: *Street Scene in New Mexico,*
MNM/DCA (NN89210)
page 60: Photo by Wyatt Davis, MNM/DCA (NN89138)
page 62: Photo by Will Connell, MNM/DCA (NN59746)
page 66: Photo by Barbara J. Harrelson
page 68: Photo by Carol Stryker, MNM/DCA (NN014248)
page 71: Photo by Will Connell, MNM/DCA (NN059757)
page 72: Photo by T. Harmon Parkhurst, MNM/DCA (NN54316)
page 75: MNM/DCA (NN27852)
page 83: Photo by Barbara J. Harrelson

Index

Abbey, Edward, 80
  The Brave Cowboy, 80
Acequia Madre and Don Miguel (9) [#2],
  52–53, 77–79
Acequia Madre to Camino del Monte Sol
  (6) [#2], 52–53, 65–67
Acquired Motives: A Dr. Sylvia Strange Novel, 58
Adams, Ansel, 63, 69
Adolph Bandelier's Home (13) [#2], 10, 84
All Aboard for Santa Fe: Railway Promotion of the
  Southwest, 1890s, 41
All the Pretty Horses, 80
Allá: Libros, Arte, Musica, 105
Ambush at Blanco Canyon, 78
American Academy of Arts and Letters, 62
American Folklore Society, 31
Anaya, Rudolfo, xii, 11, 59, 93, 94, 108
  Bless me, Ultima, 93
  Rio Grande Fall, 59
  Serafina's Stories, 11
  Shaman Winter, 59
  Zia Summer, 59
Ancient Child, The, 32
And Now, Miguel, 80
Ancient City Book Shop/Press, 30, 31, 99
Applegate, Frank, 68, 70, 73
  Native Tales of New Mexico, 6
Arkin, Alan, xii
Arroyo Tenorio to Acequia Madre (5)
  [#2], 52–53, 64–65
Atchison, Topeka, and Santa Fe Railway, 25, 40
Auden, W. H., 63
Austin, Mary Hunter, xii, 26, 35, 52–53, 55, 63,
  67–70, **68,** 73
  The Children Sing in the Far West, 69
  The Land of Journeys' Ending, 67
  Native Tales of New Mexico (intro), 69
  Starry Adventure, 67
"Authors and Books in Colonial New Mexico," 8
Azro Press, 98

Baca, Elfego, 19, 79
Baca, Elmo, 74
  Mabel's Santa Fe and Taos: Bohemian
    Legends, 1900–1950, 74
Baca, Jimmy Santiago, 93
Baca, Sonny, 59

Bachrach, Arthur, 97
Bakos, Josef, 76
Bandelier, Adolph, 9–10, 23, 83, 84
  The Delight Makers, 84
Bandelier National Monument, 10, 84
Barcelo, Gertrudis. *See* La Doña Tules
Barrio de Analco (1) [#2], 52–53, 54–55, 56
Baumann, Gustave, 63; cover woodcut by, iv
Beck & Pault, map detail, **17,** 123
"Behind Adobe Walls" (tour), 65
Behind Adobe Walls: The Hidden Homes and
    Gardens of Santa Fe and Taos, 25
Beloved House, The, 70
Ben Hur: A Tale of the Christ, 16, 23
Big Country, The, 78–79
Billy the Kid, 18–21, 46
Billy the Kid Rides Again: Digging for the Truth, 21
Bingham, Sallie, xii
Bishop's Lodge Ranch Resort & Spa, 84
Blacker, Irwin R., 11
  Taos, A Novel, 11
Bless Me, Ultima, 93
Blood and Thunder: An Epic of the American West, 20
Bloom, Claire, 77
Bluestone, Debora, 103
Bohr, Niels, 29
Bolton, Ralph, 59
Bonney, William H. *See* Billy the Kid
Bookstores/newsstands, featured:
    Collected Works Bookstore (B4), 46, 105
    Downtown Subscription (B1), 65
    Garcia Street Books (B1), 65, 106
    La Fonda Newsstand (B3), 39
    Nicholas Potter Bookseller (B2), 31, 107
    Palace Gift Shop (B1), 21
Borins, Edward and Eva, 106
Bow, Clara, 63
Bradbury-Reid, Ellen, ix, 101
Bradford, Richard, 42, 77–78, 80, 94
  Red Sky at Morning, 42, 77–78, 80
  So Far from Heaven, 78
Brujas, Bultos, y Brasas: Tales of Witchcraft and the
    Supernatural in the Pecos Valley, 49
Burro Alley (8) [#1], 2, 3, 44–46, **45,** 47, 81
Bryan, Howard, 19
  Incredible Elfego Baca, The: Good Man,
    Bad Man of the Old West, 19

Burrito Company building, 24

Bursum, Holm, Senator/Bursum Bill, 68, 69

*But Time and Chance: The Story of Padre
    Martinez of Taos, 1793–1867,* 37

Butch Cassidy and the Sundance Kid, 79

Bynner, Witter "Hal," xii, 26, 38, 52–53,
        59–64, **60, 62,** 73
    Journey with Genius, 61
    photo by, **27,** 123

Café Pasqual's, 48

Camino Real, 5

Canyon Road (11) [#2], x, 26, 30, 53, 66,
        77, 81–84

Carmelite Monastery & Immaculate Heart of
    Mary Retreat and Conference Center, 70

Carson, Christopher "Kit," 20

Casa Querida, 67

Cassidy, Gerald, 52–53, 69, 80–81

Cassidy, Ina Sizer, 80

Catcher in the Rye, 77

**Cathedral Basilica of St. Francis of Assisi
    (6) [#1],** 2, 3, **33,** 33–35, 48

Cather, Willa, xii, 30, 33–35, 37, 63, 96
    Death Comes for the Archbishop, 33, 34, 37

Catholic Church, 35, 37

Catron & Elkins, 18

Catron, Thomas B., 18

Center of Arts and Cultural Studies, IAIA, 32

Centuries of Santa Fe, The, 35

Chapel of Our Lady of Light, 50

Chávez, Angélico, Fray, xii, **22**–23, 37, 94
    *But Time and Chance: The Story of Padre
        Martinez of Taos, 1793–1867,* 37
    *My Penitente Land: Reflections on Spanish
        New Mexico,* 23
    *Origins of New Mexico Families: A Genealogy
        of the Spanish Colonial Period,* 23

Chávez, Denise, 98

Chávez, Manuel, 22

Chávez, Thomas, 23

Chiaroscuro Contemporary Art, 52–53, 67

Children Sing in the Far West, The, 69

Christian Brothers, 56

Church, Peggy Pond, 28–29
    *The House at Otowi Bridge: The Story of
        Edith Warner and Los Alamos,* 28–29

City of Holy Faith, xii, 13, 25, 35

Clear Light Publishers, 98

Cleaveland, Agnes Morley, 20
    No Life for a Lady, 20

Cohen, Saul, 11

Colfax County War, 18

Collected Works Bookstore (B4) [#1],
        2, 3, 46, 105

College of Santa Fe, 56

Collier, John, 96

Columbia Literary History of the United States, 7

Commerce of the Prairies, 14

Community Theater of Santa Fe, 55

Compound Restaurant, The, 82

Conant, Jennet, 28
    *109 East Palace: Robert Oppenheimer
        and the Secret City of Los Alamos,* 28

Connell, Evan, xii, 20
    *Son of the Morning Star: Custer and the
        Little Bighorn,* 20

Connell, Will, photos by, **43, 62, 71,** 123

Conquest of Don Pedro, The, 44

"Contemporary Mystery Writers," 58

"Controversy and Reform," 35–38

"Conversion of Cletus Xywanda, The," 13–14

Cook, Mary Straw, 50
    *Loretto, The Sisters and Their Santa Fe
        Chapel,* 50

Coyote Waits, 80

Crawford, Stanley G., 67
    *Mayordomo: Chronicle of an Acequia in
        Northern New Mexico,* 67

Creative Cities Network, x

Creative City, x. *See also* Santa Fe

Croft, Joshua, 59

Cuaderno de Ortigrafia, 14

Cui Bono? (Who Benefits?), 81

Custer, George Armstrong, 20, 48

Curtis, Edward T., 24

D. H. Lawrence Ranch (Kiowa Ranch), 96, 109

Dancing Gods, 43

Daniel Martin, 14

Davey, Randall, 81

Davis, W. W. H., 89
    El Gringo, or New Mexico and Her People, 89

Davis, Wyatt, photo by, **60,** 123

De La Peña House, 70

Death Comes for the Archbishop, 33, 34, 37

Death of a Citizen, 78

Delight Makers, The, 84

Dennis, Landt, and Lisl Dennis, 25
    *Behind Adobe Walls: The Hidden Homes
        and Gardens of Santa Fe and Taos,* 25

Desperate Silence, A, 58

Distant Trumpet, A, 38, 80

Dingee, Tyler, photos by, **33, 41,** 123

Dobie, J. Frank, ii
  Guide to Life and Literature of the
    Southwest, ii
Donahue, Troy, 38
Dorothy Doyle's Reading Sampler, 98
Douglas, Melvyn, 19
Down the Santa Fe Trail and into Mexico: The
  Diary of Susan Shelby Magoffin, 1846–47, 12
Downtown Subscription (B1) [#2], 65
Downtown Santa Fe [Walk #1], x, 2–5
Doyle, Arthur Conan, Sir, 59
Dudzik, Andy, 105
Dumont, Andre and Carol, 106
Dumont Maps & Books of the West, 106
Duncan, Isadora, 63
Dunne, B. B. (Brian Boru), **41**, 42, 65
Duvall, Robert, 41
Dye, Victoria, 41
  All Aboard for Santa Fe: Railway
    Promotion of the Southwest, 1890s, 41

Easy Rider, 79
Eisenhardt, Gae E., 98
El Gringo, or New Mexico and Her People, 89
el norte, 34, 67
El Palacio, 103
El Zaguán (12) [#2], 53, 82–83, **83**
Elkins, Stephen, 18
Ellis, Fremont, 76
Escapade, 59
Essence of Santa Fe, The: From a Way of Life
  to a Style, 25
Evans, John, 73
Evans, Max, 80
  Hi-Lo Country, The, 80
Exchange Hotel, 40
Exiles and Fabrications, 76

Facing Southwest: The Life and Houses of John
  Gaw Meem, 25
Fair God, The, 16
Fergusson, Erna, xii, 42, **43**, 93
  Dancing Gods, 43
  New Mexico: A Pageant of Three Peoples, 43
Fergusson, Harvey, 19, 44
  The Conquest of Don Pedro, 44
  Footloose McGarnigal, 44
  Grant of Kingdom, 19, 44
  Wolf Song, 44
Fiesta Melodrama, 55
Fifteen Club, The, 90
"Films Based on New Mexico Literature," 79–80

Fiore, Kyle, xiii
  Santa Fe and Taos: The Writer's Era,
    1916–1941, xiii
First Blood, 59
Flower in the Desert, A, 59
Fly on the Wall, The, 58, 80
Flynn, Errol, 41, 48, 63
"Folklorist as Publisher, The," 31
Folsom, Franklin, 11
  Indian Uprising on the Rio Grande:
    The Pueblo Revolt of 1680, 11
  Red Power on the Rio Grande: The Native
    American Revolution of 1680, 11
Footloose McGarnigal, 44
Four Faces West, 79
Fowles, John, 14
  Daniel Martin, 14
Franciscan friars, 8, 9
Frank Waters Foundation, 95, 109
Fray Angélico Chávez History Library
  (3) [#1], 2, 3, 10, 14, **22**, 22–26
  Photo Archives, 23
"From Novel to Big Screen: Films Based on
  New Mexico Literature," 79–80
Frost, Robert, 59
Frost, Robert (poet), 63

Gallegos, Anna, 100
García, Nasario, 49
  Brujas, Bultos, y Brasas: Tales of Witchcraft
    and the Supernatural in the Pecos Valley, 49
Garcia Street Books (B1) [#2], 65, 106
Garland, Judy, 47
Garrett, Pat F., 19, 21
Garson, Greer, 41
Gerald Cassidy Placita (10) [#2],
  52–53, 80–81
Gerónimo, 82
Gibbs Smith, Publisher, 99
Girard, Alexander, 82
Goldberg, Julia, 105
Golden Age of Arts and Letters, xii
Gothic Revival style, 34
Graham, Martha, 63
Gran Via Publications, 103
Grant of Kingdom, 19, 44
Grant, Ulysses S., General and Mrs., 41
Grapes of Wrath, The, 79
Great River: The Story of the Rio Grande in
  North American History, 38
Great Taos Bank Robbery and Other Indian
  Country Affairs, The, 13–14

Greek Revival features, 24
Green Grow the Lilacs, 79
Gregg, Josiah, 14
    Commerce of the Prairies, 14
Grimes, Martha, 58–59
    Rainbow's End, 59
Grusin, Dave, 57
Gunstock Hill Books, 106
Guide to Life and Literature of the Southwest, ii
Gutiérrez, Ramón, 10–11
    *When Jesus Came, the Corn Mothers Went
        Away,* 10–11

Habit of Empire, The, 38
Hackman, Gene, xii
Hamel, Neil, 59
Hamilton, Donald, 78
    Ambush at Blanco Canyon, 78
    The Big Country, 78–79
    Death of a Citizen, 78
Hammett, Jerilou, 25
    *The Essence of Santa Fe: From a Way
        of Life to a Style,* 25
Hammett, Kingsley, 25
    *The Essence of Santa Fe: From a Way
        of Life to a Style,* 25
Harrelson, Barbara J., photos by,
    47, 66, 83, 123
Harris, Lisa, 107
Harvey, Fred, 40–41
Harvey Girls, The: Women Who Opened the West, 41
Harvey House(s), 41, 42
Harveycars, **40,** 42
Havilland, Olivia de, 48
Hayes, Joe (storyteller), 99
Hayes, Rutherford B., Mrs., 41
Hayes, Rutherford B., President, 18, 41
Hayworth, Rita, 47, 63
Helm, Matt, 78
Hemingway, Ernest, 59
Henderson Evans, Alice, 73
Henderson, Alice Corbin, ix, xii, 61,
    70–72, **71,** 73
    Red Earth: Poems of New Mexico, 73
Henderson, William Penhallow "Whippy,"
    70, **71,** 72–73
Henry, O., 63
Hepburn, Katharine, 19
Hercules, task of, 18
Hermit's Peak, 58
Heston, Charlton, 16, 79
Hi-Lo Country, The, 80

Hillerman, Ann, 103
Hillerman, Tony, xii, 13–14, 58, 76, 80, 109
    "The Conversion of Cletus Xywanda,"
        13–14
    Coyote Waits, 80
    The Fly on the Wall, 58
    *The Great Taos Bank Robbery and
        Other Indian Country Affairs,* 13–14
    Skinwalkers, 80
    A Thief of Time, 80
Historia de la Nueva México, 9, 10, 23
"Historic Preservation and Santa Fe Style," 24–26
Historic Preservation Award, 60
Historic Santa Fe Foundation, 26, 55, 82
    Old Santa Fe Today, 82
Historical Society of New Mexico, 27
History and Government of New Mexico, 18
History Museum, Museum of New Mexico, 15
Homer/"Homeric" epic, xiii, 10
Horgan, Paul, xii, 37, 38, 61, 65, 73–74, 80, 94
    The Centuries of Santa Fe, 38
    A Distant Trumpet, 38, 80
    *Great River: The Story of the Rio Grande in
        North American History,* 38
    The Habit of Empire, 38
    Lamy of Santa Fe: His Life and Times, 37
    Tracings: A Book of Partial Portraits, 73–74
Hotel St. Francis, 48
Hough, Emerson, 18
Houghton, Harmon, 98
*House at Otowi Bridge, The: The Story of Edith
    Warner and Los Alamos,* 28–29
House Made of Dawn, 32, 80
Houseman, A. E., 63
Hughes, Dorothy Belle Flanagan, 5–6, 79
    In a Lonely Place, 6
    The Fallen Sparrow, 6
    Ride the Pink Horse, 5, 79
Huning, Franz, 44
Hunt, Robert, 63
Hurd, Peter, 38
Huxley, Aldous, 63

Iliad, The, touring productions of, xiii
*Incredible Elfego Baca, The: Good Man, Bad Man
    of the Old West,* 19
Indian Detours, 40, 42, 43
*Indian Uprising on the Rio Grande: The Pueblo
    Revolt of 1680,* 11
indigenous peoples, heritage of, 6
Inn at Loretto, 49
Inn at the End of the Trail, **39**

Inn of the Anasazi, 24
Inn of the Turquoise Bear, 52–53, 60
"Inspired by Santa Fe," 13
Institute of American Indian Arts (IAIA), xii, 31, 32
International Folk Art Museum, 82
Isherwood, Christopher, 63

James, Henry, 63
Jemez Mountains, 77
Jemez Pueblo, 32
Johnson, James L., 83
Johnson, Samuel, 1
Johnson, Willard "Spud," xiii, 30
Journey with Genius, 61
Jury, Richard, 59

Kadlec, Robert, 30–31
Kagel, Katherine, 48
Kanon, Joseph, 58
    Los Alamos, 58
Keaton, Diane, 41
Keegan, Marcia, 98
Kempes, Lesley Poling, 41
    The Harvey Girls: Women Who Opened the West, 41
Kerney, Kevin, 58
Kid Antrim. *See* Billy the Kid
Krumgold, Joseph, 80
    And Now, Miguel, 80

La Casa Adobe, 31
La Doña Tules, 45–46
La Farge, John Pen, 42, 78
    Turn Left at the Sleeping Dog, 42, 78
La Farge, Oliver, xii, 13, 42, 46, 63, 69, 92
    Laughing Boy: A Navajo Love Story, 63
    Santa Fe: The Autobiography of a Southwestern Town, 64
La Fonda Hotel (7) [#1], 2, 3, 6, 30, **39**, 39–44, **40**, 41–42, **72**, 84
La Fonda Newsstand (B3) [#1], 2, 3, 39
La Herencia, 103
La Llorona (the Wailing Woman), 4
La Villa Real de Santa Fe, 4
Lamy, Jean Baptiste, Archbishop, 34–38, 84, 97
    Lamy of Santa Fe: His Life and Times, 37
Land of Enchantment: Memoirs of Marian Russell Along the Santa Fe Trail: As Dictated to Mrs. Hal Russell, 12
Land of Journeys' Ending, The, 67
Land of Poco Tiempo, 90
Land of the Pueblos, The, 13

Lane, Nancy, 30
Lannan Foundation, 48, 94, 99
Laughing Boy: A Navajo Love Story, 63
Laughlin, Ruth, xii, 46
    Wind Leaves No Shadow, The, 46
Lawrence, D. H., xiii, 61, 73, 74, 96
Lawrence, Frieda, 61, 73, 96
Lensic Performing Arts Center, 47, 99
Lensic Theater (9) [#1], 2, 3, **47**, 47–49
Lew Wallace: An Autobiography, 17
Lewis, Henry, 106
Life of Gen. Ben Harrison, The, 16–17
Lincoln County War, 18, 19
Lindbergh, Charles, 41
"Links Between the Writers and Artists of Santa Fe and Taos," 73
Literacy Volunteers of Santa Fe, 100
Lonely Are the Brave, 80
López, Gerónimo (Jerome), 82
Lore of New Mexico, The, 93
Lorenzo in Taos, 74
Loretto Chapel (11) [#1], 2, 3, 34, 50, **51**
Loretto, The Sisters and Their Santa Fe Chapel, 50
Los Alamos, 58
Los Alamos, New Mexico, 27–29, 77, 84
Los Cinco Pintores, 70, 74, 75
los hermanos, 36
Lovett, Sarah, xii, 58
    Acquired Motives: A Dr. Sylvia Strange Novel, 58
    A Desperate Silence, 58
Luce, Henry and Clare Boothe, 41
Luhan, Mabel Dodge, ix, xiii, 61, 73–74, 95–96
    Lorenzo in Taos, 74
    Winter in Taos, 74
Luhan, Tony, 96
Lummis, Charles, 90
    The Land of Poco Tiempo, 90
Lumpkins, William, 31
    La Casa Adobe, 31

Mabel Dodge Luhan: New Woman, New Worlds, 74
Mabel Dodge Luhan House, 95–96, 109
Mabel's Santa Fe and Taos: Bohemian Legends, 1900–1950, 74
Mafchir, Jim, 103
Magoffin, Susan, 12
    Down the Santa Fe Trail and into Mexico: Diary of Susan Shelby Magoffin, 1846–47, 12
Man Who Killed the Deer, The, 95
Manhattan Project, 27–29, 58
Marin, John, 96
Martin, Dean, 78

Martin, Robin M., 105

Martínez, Antonio José, Padre, 14, 35, 37–38, 89
    Cuaderno de Ortigrafia, 14
    statue of, 97

Mary Austin's Home (7) [#2], 52–53, 67–70
Mary Hunter Austin, 70
Masked Gods: Navajo and Pueblo Ceremonialism, 95
Masquerade, 59
Massey, Dorothy, 106
Mather, Christine, 25
    Santa Fe Style, 25
Maxwell, Lucien Bonaparte, 19
Mayer, Bob, xii
Mayordomo: Chronicle of an Acequia in Northern
    New Mexico, 67
McCarthy, Cormac, xii, 80
    All the Pretty Horses, 80
McCarty, Henry. *See* Billy the Kid
McGarrity, Michael, xii, 57–58
    Hermit's Peak, 58
    Nothing But Trouble, 58
    Serpent Gate, 57
    Tularosa, 58
McGraw, Ali, xii
McKibben, Dorothy, 27
Meem, John Gaw, 26, 71
Menuhin, Yehudi, 47
Mera, Frank, Dr., 70
Meridian: A Novel of Kit Carson's West, 20
Mexican War, 18
Mexico, Republic of, 11–12, 3
Milagro Beanfield War, The, 57, 80, 95
Miller, Jay, 21
    Billy the Kid Rides Again:
        Digging for the Truth, 21
"Miraculous Staircase," 50, **51**
Moby Dickens Bookshop, 96–97
Momaday, N. Scott, xii, 7, 32, 80, 108
    The Ancient Child, 32
    House Made of Dawn, 32, 80
    The Names: A Memoir, 32
    "The Native Voice," 7
    The Way to Rainy Mountain, 32
Moorish-Spanish architecture, 24, 48
Morrell, David, 59
    First Blood, 59
    Nightscape, 59
Morris, Ashleigh, 104
Mruk, Wladyslaw (Walter), 76
Museum Hill, 82
Museum of Fine Arts, 73, 75, 81
Museum of New Mexico, History Museum,
    15, 103

Museum of New Mexico Press, 100
Museum of the Institute of American
    Indian Arts (5) [#1], 2, 3, 31–32
My Life on the Frontier, 1864–1882, 19
My Nine Years as Governor of the Territory of New
    Mexico, 19
My Penitente Land: Reflections on Spanish New
    Mexico, 23
Myth of Santa Fe, The: The Creation of a Modern
    Regional Tradition, 25

Names, The: A Memoir, 32
Nash, Willard, 76
National Hispanic Cultural Center, 23
National Museum, Mexico, 10
National Register of Historic Places, 96
Native American Fine Art, 31
Native Americans, 4 (fn1), 7
Native Tales of New Mexico, 6
"Native Voice, The," 7
New Mexican column (Dunne), 42
New Mexico: A Pageant of Three Peoples, 43
New Mexico Association on Indian Affairs, 68
New Mexico Book Association, 100
New Mexico Capitol (3) [#2], 52–53, 57–58
New Mexico Magazine, 57, 104
New Mexico Mission style, 55
New Mexico Military Institute (NMMI), 38
New Mexico Style: A Sourcebook of Traditional
    Architectural Details, 25
New Mexico Territory, 16–18, 26. 34, 36
New Spain, 5
Nicholas Potter Bookseller (B2) [#1],
    2, 3, 31, 107
Nichols, John, 57, 80, 05
    The Milagro Beanfield War, 57, 80, 95
Nightscape, 59
Nine Lives of Elfego Baca, The, 79
No Life for a Lady, 20
Nobel Prize in Literature, 95
Nolan, Frederick W., 19
    Pat F. Garrett's Authentic Life of
        Billy, the Kid, 19
    West of Billy, the Kid, The, 19
North of the Border, 59
Nothing But Trouble, 58
Nusbaum, Jesse L. 24

109 East Palace, 27–29
109 East Palace: Robert Oppenheimer and the
    Secret City of Los Alamos, 28
O'Brien, Edna, 108
O'Keeffe, Georgia, 63, 74, 96

O'Neill, Eugene, 74
Oates, Joyce Carol, 108
Ocean Tree Books, 100
Odyssey, The, touring productions of, xiii
Oklahoma! 79
Old Man Gloom 74–75, **75**
Old Santa Fe Association, 26, 68
Old Santa Fe Today, 82, 84
**Old Santa Fe Trail to Canyon Road
    [Walk #2],** 52–84
Oñate, Juan de,
Oppenheimer: J. Robert, 27–29, 63; Kitty, 29
*Origins of New Mexico Families: A Genealogy of
    the Spanish Colonial Period,* 23
Otero, Miguel Antonio, 16, 19
    My Life on the Frontier, 1864–1882, 19
    *My Nine Years as Governor of the Territory
        of New Mexico,* 19
"Other Neighbors on the Camino," 70–73
Other Side of Death, The, 59

Pacheco, Ana, 104
Page, Jake, 58
    The Stolen Gods, 58
Pajarito Plateau, ancient peoples of, 84
Palace Gift Shop (B3) [#1], 2, 3, 21
**Palace of the Governors, The (2) [#1],
    15,** 15–21
Palace of the Governors 2, 3, 4, 8, 14, 23,
    26–27, 37, 54, 71, 123
    "Paper Soul: Indigenous Bookcrafts
        of Mexico," 8
    Photo Archives, 23, 12
Parkhurst, T. Harmon, 24; photos by,
    39, 51, 72, 123
Pasatiempo, xiii, 30. 104
Pat F. Garrett's Authentic Life of Billy, the Kid, 19
PBS Mystery Series, 80
Pearce, T. M., 70
    The Beloved House, 70
    Mary Hunter Austin, 70
Peck, Gregory, 79
Pecos Pueblo, 81
PEN, New Mexico, 101
Penitentes, Penitente Brothers, 23, 36
Pizarro, and conquistadors, 8
Plaza, The (1) [#1], 2, 3, 4–14, **6,** 30, **40**
Poetry magazine, 72
Polese, Richard, 100
Popé (San Juan Pueblo medicine man), 11
Pound, Ezra, 63
Priestly, J. B., 63
Prince and Sena Plazas (4) [#1], 2, 3, 26–31

Prince Plaza, 26
Prince, L. Bradford, 16, 26–27
    Spanish Mission Churches of New Mexico, 27
Publisher's Weekly, 28
Pueblo Independence Day, 4 (fn1)
Pueblos/Pueblo peoples, 10, 28, 69, 84
Pueblo Revolt of 1680, The, 4, 9, 10, 11, 54, 55
Pulitzer Prize, 32, 37, 38, 63

Rafael Borrego House, 82
Rainbow's End, 58
Rambo, 59
Randall Davey Audubon Center, 81
Read More About . . .
    "Contemporary Mystery Writers," 58
    "The Pueblo Revolt of 1680," 11
    "Santa Fe Style," 25
    "The Wild West and New Mexico
        Territory," 19–20
Readings and Conversations, 48, 99
Reagan, Ronald, 48
Recursos de Santa Fe, ix, 100, 108
Red Earth: Poems of New Mexico, 73
*Red Power on the Rio Grande: The Native
    American Revolution of 1680,* 11
Red Sky at Morning, 42, 80
Redford, Robert, 57
Reed, John (Jack), 74
Rhodes, Eugene Manlove, 79
    Pasó por Aquí (They Passed This Way), 79
Richter, Conrad, 19, 79
    Sea of Grass, The, 19, 79
Ride the Pink Horse, 5, 79
Riggs, Lynn, 79
    Green Grow the Lilacs, 79
Rio Grande Fall, 59
Robey, Roberta, 30
Rogers, Roy, 47
Romanesque style, 33
"Roundhouse, the," 52–53, 57–58
Rudnick, Lois Palken, 74
    *Mabel Dodge Luhan: New Woman,
        New Worlds,* 74
Russell, Marian Sloan, 12
    *Land of Enchantment: Memoirs of Marian
        Russell Along the Santa Fe Trail:
        As Dictated to Mrs. Hal Russell,* 12

San Ildefonso Pueblo, 28
San José Bell, 56
San Juan Pueblo, 9, 11
San Miguel Mission Chapel (2) [#2],
    ii, 52–53, 54, 55–57, **56**

Sandburg, Carl, 63
Sangre de Cristo mountains, 81
Santa Fe, a bird's-eye view of, **17**
Santa Fe and Taos: The Writer's Era, 1916–1941, xiii
Santa Fe Farmers Market, 67
Santa Fe Fiesta, 5, **6**, 75
Santa Fe Film Festival, 108
Santa Fe Garden Club, 65
   "Behind Adobe Walls," 65
Santa Fe New Mexican, The, xiii, 21, 30,
   64, 69, 104
Santa Fe Opera, 48, 102
Santa Fe Players/Playhouse, 55
Santa Fe Reporter, 105
Santa Fe Ring, 18
Santa Fe River Walk (10) [#1], 2, 3, 48, 49
Santa Fe Short Story Festival, 108
Santa Fe Style, xiii, 24–26
"Santa Fe Style," 25
Santa Fe Style, 25
Santa Fe: Autobiography of a Southwestern Town, 64
Santa Fe Trail, 48
Santa Fe Trail, 12, 14, 39, 46, 83
Santa Fe Writers Conference, 108
Santuario de Chimayó, 68
SAR Press, 101
Satterthwait, Walter, 59
   Escapade, 59
   A Flower in the Desert, 59
   Masquerade, 59
   A Wall of Glass, 59
   Wilde West, 59
Saturday Review of Literature, 69–70
Scholz, Peter, 25
   *The Essence of Santa Fe: From a Way
   of Life to a Style,* 25
School of American Research, 101
Scott, Winfield Townley, 76
   Exiles and Fabrications, 76
Sea of Grass, The, 10, 79
Second Pueblo Revolt, 69
Sena Plaza, 26, **27**, 29–31
Serafina's Stories, 11
Sergeant, Elizabeth Shepley, 70
Serpent Gate, 57
Seton, Ernest Thompson, **68**
Shaefer, Jack, 20
   Shane, 20
Shaman Winter, 59
Sherman Asher Publishing, 102
Sheppard, Carl, photo by, **15**, 123
Sherwood's Spirit of America, 53, 84
Shuster, Will, 74–75, **75**

Sides, Hampton, xii, 20
   *Blood and Thunder: An Epic of the
   American West,* 20
Silkwood, 79
Simmons, Marc, 8, 10, 93
   "Authors and Books in Colonial
   New Mexico," 8, 10
Sisters of Loretto, 50
Skinwalkers, 80
Sloan, John, 74
Smith, James Clois, 102
Society of the Muse of the Southwest, 109
So Far from Heaven, 78
S.O.M.O.S., 109
*Son of the Morning Star: Custer and the Little
   Bighorn,* 20
*Southwest Crossroads: Cultures and Histories
   of the American Southwest,* 101
Southwest Literary Center, ix, 108
Southwest Media, LLC, 104
Southwestern Association for Indian Art, 68
Spanish Colonial Arts Society, 68
Spanish Colonial elements, 5, 10, 13, 14
Spanish Mission Churches of New Mexico, 27
Spanish Pueblo/Revival style, 24, 33, 49, 70, 73
Spell of New Mexico, The, 76
Spender, Stephen, 63
St. John's College, 63, 102
St. John's College Library & Fine Arts Guild, 102
St. Joseph the Carpenter, 50
St. Michael's College, 34, 56
St. Vincent Millay, Edna, 63
St. Vincent's Hospital, 34
Starry Adventure, 67
Stein, Gertrude, 74
Stewart, James, 41
Stieglitz, Alfred, 74
"Stitch and Bitch, The" (women's club), 13
Stolen Blue, The, 59
Stolen Gods, The, 58
"Storytelling Traditions of Three Peoples," 6–14
Strange, Sylvia, Dr., 58
Stravinsky, Igor, 63
Stryker, Carol, photo by, **68**, 123
Summer Classics in Santa Fe, 102
Sunmount Sanitarium, 61, 70, 71
Sunstone Press, 102
SWAIA, 68
Sze, Arthur, xii

Tammany Hall, 26
Territorial style, 24, 33
Taos, A Novel, 11

Taos artists/writers, xii–xiii, 14, 35, 38, 68, 73, 95
Taos Pueblo, 69, 95, 96
Taos Society of Artists, 76
Taos Summer Writers' Conference, 109
Thief of Time, A, 80
Thomas, Richard, 77
Tlaxcalan Indians, 54, 55
Tio Vivo, 5
Tony Hillerman Writers Conference, 108
Tracings: A Book of Partial Portraits, 73–74
Tracy, Spencer, 19
Trapp Family Singers, 47
Travel Bug Coffee Shop, 107
Travolta, John, 41
True Believers Comics & Gallery, 107
Tularosa, 58
Turn Left at the Sleeping Dog, 42, 78
Turner, Frederick, xii
Twain, Mark, 63

UNESCO, x
United Way, 5
University of New Mexico, 96
University of New Mexico Press, 102
Upper Canyon Road, 81
U.S. Hotel, 40

Van Gieson, Judith, 59
    North of the Border, 59
    The Other Side of Death, 59
    The Stolen Blue, 59
    Vanishing Point, 59
Varjabedian, Craig, 36
    *En Divina Luz: The Penitente Moradas
        of New Mexico,* 36
Vaughn, John H. 18
    History and Government of New Mexico, 18
Video Library Inc., 107
Vierra, Carlos, 71
Villa, Pancho, 19
Villagra Book Shop, **27,** 30–31
Villagrá, Gaspar Pérez de, Captain, 9, **9,** 23
    Historia de la Nueva México, 9, 10, 23
Visitor Center, New Mexico State, 57
*Voices from the Southwest: A Gathering of Poetry,
    Essays, and Art . . . Lawrence Clark Powell,* 8

Wall of Glass, A, 59
Wallace, Lewis "Lew," 16–18, 21, 37, 57
    Ben Hur: A Tale of the Christ, 16
    The Fair God, 16
    Lew Wallace: An Autobiography, 17
    The Life of Gen. Ben Harrison, 16–17

Wallace, Susan Elston, 13, 17–18
    The Land of the Pueblos, 13, 17
Wallis, Michael, 36
    *En Divina Luz: The Penitente Moradas
        of New Mexico,* 36
Warner, Edith, 28–29
Warren, Nancy Hunter, 25
    *New Mexico Style: A Sourcebook
        of Traditional Architectural Details,* 25
Waters, Frank, xiii, 94, 95
    The Man Who Killed the Deer, 95
    *Masked Gods: Navajo and Pueblo
        Ceremonialism,* 95
Way to Rainy Mountain, The, 32
Weigle, Marta, xiii, 31
    "The Folklorist as Publisher," 31
    The Lore of New Mexico, 93
    *Santa Fe and Taos: The Writer's Era,
        1916–1941,* xiii
West of Billy, the Kid, The, 19
West, The (PBS series), 32
Western Edge Press/Sherman Asher
    Publishing, 102
Wheelright Museum, 32, 99
When Jesus Came, the Corn Mothers Went Away, 10
"Wild West and New Mexico Territory, The,"
    19–20
Wilde, Oscar, 59
Wilde West, 59
Wilder, Thornton, 41, 63
Will Shuster's Home (8) [#2], 52–53, 74–77
Wilson, Chris, 25
    *Facing Southwest: The Life and Houses
        of John Gaw Meem,* 25
    *The Myth of Santa Fe: Creation of a Modern
        Regional Tradition,* 25
Wilson, Luther, 102
Wilson, Woodrow, President, 84
Wind Leaves No Shadow, The, 46
Winter in Taos, 74
Witter Bynner Foundation for Poetry, 63
Witter Bynner's Home (4) [#2], 52–53,
    59–64, **60.** *See also* Bynner, Witter "Hal"
Wolf Song, 44
Woods, Sharon, 25
    Santa Fe Style, 25
Works Progress Administration (WPA), 72
WorldHarvest Writers Workshops, 103, 109

Zia Summer, 59
Zollinger, Norman, 20
    Meridian: A Novel of Kit Carson's West, 20
Zozobra (Old Man Gloom), 74–75, **75**